eastern
wisdom
for western
minds

eastern wisdom *for* western minds

Victor M. Parachin

Drawings by Jason K. Dy

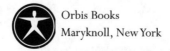

Orbis Books

Maryknoll, New York

Founded in 1970, Orbis Books endeavors to publish works that enlighten the mind, nourish the spirit, and challenge the conscience. The publishing arm of the Maryknoll Fathers and Brothers, Orbis seeks to explore the global dimensions of the Christian faith and mission, to invite dialogue with diverse cultures and religious traditions, and to serve the cause of reconciliation and peace. The books published reflect the views of their authors and do not represent the official position of the Maryknoll Society. To learn more about Maryknoll and Orbis Books, please visit our website at www.maryknoll.org.

Library of Congress Cataloging-in-Publication Data

Parachin, Victor M.
  Eastern wisdom for western minds / Victor M. Parachin.
    p. cm.
 ISBN 978-1-57075-738-9
1. Asia—Religion. 2. Philosophy, Asian. 3. Wisdom—Religious aspects. I. Title.
BL1033.P37 2007
  200.95—dc22
                       2007018117

CONTENTS

INTRODUCTION

Today there is a rampant hunger and thirst for deeper ways of living and being, particularly in North America and Western Europe. There are two reasons for this yearning. First, it may be the result of an unprecedented materialism. We have larger homes, more expensive cars, greater levels of education, and the ability to access an ever increasing number of goods and services. Second, it may be due to the increasing presence and visibility of other households of faith. There are, across the North American religious landscape, Zen centers, Buddhist cloisters, Hindu temples, Taoist study groups, and countless classes offered in Eastern religion and philosophy.

As a result of these two converging factors, more and more Western people are turning to Eastern wisdom to guide them in the restructuring and deepening of their spirituality. There is a greater appreciation for spiritual interdependence and a growing conviction that the teachings of Christianity can be energized by many insights of the Eastern religions. Many are discovering that we don't need to be of one mind to be of one heart. Placing the focus on what unites us, rather than what divides us, is beneficial for spiritual growth and evolution. This little book, laid out alphabetically, is the culmination of my own reading, research, and study of what the East has to offer us in the West.

In putting this book together, I have been guided greatly by two insights from

Eastern mystics. The first one comes from the Urdu poet and Hindu philosopher Harish Johari (1934-1999), who succinctly but profoundly observed: "If you feel you are not enlightened, you can always try to be." The other comes from J. Krishnamurti (1895-1986), who was born in South India and educated in England. Unwilling to adhere to any particular religion, he was masterful at blending the best of the East with the best of the West. Krishnamurti wisely taught: "To transform the world, we must begin with ourselves."

So this book is for all those who may not feel enlightened, but are sincerely willing to try to be. It is also for those activists who want to transform the world but understand that the process begins with the self. My conviction is that Eastern thought can open us up to more authentic ways of understanding and responding to the events, issues, and crises that come tumbling into our lives.

ACTIONS

SMALL ACTS CAN MAKE A BIG DIFFERENCE.

> *Do not overlook tiny good actions, thinking*
> *they are of no benefit; even tiny drops of water*
> *in the end will fill a huge vessel.*
>
> —THE BUDDHA

It's all too easy to discount our efforts and minimize our effectiveness on the planet because most of us are not creating global change—negotiating peace treaties, ending wars, discovering new vaccines, etc. Yet, the Buddha wisely reminds people not to overlook tiny good actions. Our small acts can, indeed, make a big difference. A tiny seed can, in time, produce a huge tree. A small act of compassion can relieve a great distress. The journey that covers an enormous landscape always begins with the first step. This true story from India provides an excellent example.

After Gandhi's assassination on January 30, 1948, Gandhi's followers naturally looked to a man named Vinoba Bhave as Gandhi's spiritual successor. Although Vinoba was not well known to the Indian public, Gandhi had been a great admirer of his, often commenting that Vinoba understood Gandhian thought better than he himself did. Vinoba had no desire to lead, preferring a life given to meditation and prayer. However, as violence erupted in many Indian states, Vinoba was moved to see if he could help resolve the conflict. One district, Telengana, close to where Vinoba was residing, was in the midst of a violent armed insurrection. Communist students and poor villagers united in a guerilla army to break the land monopoly of rich landlords. Their intention was to drive them out or kill them and then distribute the land more equitably. Tensions were high as guerillas managed to seize and control an area of three thousand villages. The Indian Army had been sent, adding its own campaign of terror. Each side was killing villagers suspected of supporting the other side.

Vinoba announced his intention to walk through the villages in the district of Telengana to speak with villagers. His goal was to find a way of ending the violence and restoring both justice and peace. On the third day of his walk, he was in a village that was an important Communist stronghold. Setting himself up in the courtyard of a Muslim prayer compound, Vinoba was soon receiving visitors from all factions in the village. Among his visitors was a group of forty families of landless people from the "untouchable" caste of Hindu society. Only the Communists would give them land, they explained. Could he appeal to the government to give them land instead? Land would give them hope for a future out of poverty, and would end the violence. In his heart, Vinoba knew the government would not likely give land to these untouchables. He did not know how to answer, and was troubled by their plight.

Later that afternoon, Vinoba held a prayer meeting that drew thousands of villagers from the surrounding area. There he presented the plight of the untouchables, asking if there was anyone who could help "these friends." A prominent landlord stood up, saying, "I am ready to give one hundred acres." Vinoba was stunned by the response. The "untouchables" were present, and declared that eighty acres would be sufficient.

Vinoba suddenly saw a solution to the nation's turmoil. At the close of the prayer meeting, he announced he would walk throughout the region asking for and collecting land for the landless. Thus began the movement called *Bhoodan,* or "land-gift," resulting in one of the world's largest voluntary land transfers. As Vinoba walked from village to village, he was soon collecting thousands of acres a day on behalf of the landless. By 1954, Vinoba and his associates had collected and transferred nearly four million acres of land.

That example from Vinoba Bhave reinforces the truth that small actions can deliver large results. Never buy into our cultural myths which say: "I can't make a difference" and "What's the use?" and "The problems are too big." Remember the Buddha's words: "Do not overlook tiny good actions, thinking they are of no benefit; even tiny drops of water in the end will fill a huge vessel." Add to his thought this wisdom from Mother Teresa of India: "In this life we cannot do great things. We can only do small things with great love."

ATTACHMENT

LETTING GO OF OUR ATTACHMENT TO PAIN.

The mind is its own place, and in itself can make
a heaven of hell, a hell of heaven.
—JOHN MILTON

Attachment is a major theme in Eastern thought, particularly in Buddhism. The Buddha specifically taught that it is attachment that leads to suffering. We suffer not because an unpleasant event takes place in our lives, but because we add to that event the huge burden of emotions and fantasies: anger, resentment, hostility, entitlement, fear, grief, etc. The Buddha taught that freedom from attachment is the cure for suffering. "For him who is wholly free from craving, there is no grief, much less fear." That lesson is the point of this story about an old gardener who visited a monk seeking his advice: "Great Monk, let me ask you: How can I attain liberation?" The Great Monk replied: "Who tied you up?" This old gardener answered: "Nobody tied me up." The Great Monk said: "Then why do you seek liberation?"

The point of the story is this: if you don't have attachments, then you are naturally liberated!

Here's a true story from our times and our culture that shows how suffering is released when we let go of our attachments, especially our attachment to pain. As the American poet Edwin Markham approached his retirement years, he discovered that the man to whom he had entrusted his financial portfolio had squandered all the money. Markham's dream of a comfortable retirement vanished. He began to brood over the injustice and the loss. His anger deepened. Over time, Markham's bitterness grew by leaps and bounds. One day while sitting at his table, Markham found himself drawing circles as he tried to soothe the turmoil he felt within. Finally, he concluded: "I must forgive him, and I will forgive him." Looking again at the circles he had drawn on the paper before him, Markham wrote these lines:

> *He drew a circle to shut me out,*
> *Heretic, rebel, a thing to flout;*
> *But love and I had the wit to win,*
> *We drew a circle to take him in.*

Although Markham wrote hundreds of poems contained in many volumes, the words he wrote while forgiving are his most famous and memorable. As he forgave, a torrent of creativity was released within him. Although he adhered to the Christian faith, Markham's action was also a profoundly Buddhist one. By extending forgiveness, he let go of his attachment to hatred, anger, and revenge. As long as we are unable to forgive, we remain attached to the person who hurt us. Unwilling to forgive, we linger in a permanent state of attachment to the pain caused by the offender. Eastern thought consistently reminds people that pain is inevitable, suffering is optional. Suffering is caused by our emotional reaction to our pain. We suffer when we hold on to the hurts that come our way, rather than letting them go. Milton is quite right when he says that our mind can make our lives a living hell. Forgiveness is a powerful action of releasing our attachment and neutralizing suffering.

The poets and mystics among us have long known that the act of forgiveness releases great healing power. Author Charles Filmore recommended forgiveness as the most effective way of restoring inner harmony and balance: "There is a mental treatment guaranteed to cure every ill that flesh is heir to: Sit for half an hour every night and forgive everyone against whom you have any ill will or antipathy." Extending forgiveness is one way of letting go of our emotional attachments and entanglements.

AWAKE

ARE YOU SLEEPWALKING THROUGH YOUR LIFE?

When walking, walk. When sitting, sit.
But don't wobble!
—ZEN PROVERB

It is said that soon after the Buddha experienced enlightenment, he passed a man on the road who was immediately struck by the Buddha's appearance. The Buddha had an extraordinary radiance and peacefulness about him. The man knew he was in the company of an unusual person and wanted to know more about him. Thus, he stopped and asked the Buddha:

"My friend, what are you? Are you a celestial being, or perhaps a god?"

"No," said Buddha.

"Well, then are you some kind of magician or wizard?"

"No," Buddha said again.

"Are you a man?"

"No."

"Well, my friend, what then are you?"

This time the Buddha replied, "I am awake."

One of Buddhism's great insights is that some people—perhaps too many people—are sleepwalking through their lives. Rather than be awake and live mindfully, they simply go through the motions without awareness of their activity. Many individuals operate on automatic pilot. A sad but dramatic example of this can be seen in the events that led to the 1982 crash of an Air Florida plane, which cost the lives of seventy-four passengers.

At the time, it was noted that the pilot and co-pilot were in excellent physical health. Neither was tired, stressed, or under the influence of alcohol or drugs. After the crash, an extensive investigation revealed that there was a problem with the crew's pre-takeoff control checks, which follow this pattern: As the co-pilot calls out each control on his list, the pilot makes sure the switches are where he wants them to be. One of those controls is an anti-icer. On that fateful day, the pilot and co-pilot went over each of the controls as they had always done. They went through the calls, checking "off" when the anti-icer was called. However, this time the flight was different from their usual southern routes, as a surprise winter storm hit the Washington area. It was icy outside and ice was forming on the aircraft wings. As they went through the control checks, the pilot unfortunately was on automatic pilot and kept the anti-icing switch off when he should have put it on.

Here's the point Buddhism would like us to get: There can be disastrous consequences to our living when we are not fully awake, aware, and engaged with the daily events of our lives. Many people live unfulfilled, unhappy lives because they blindly follow routines or simply do what is expected. As a result they remain in jobs and relationships that are not only meaningless but even toxic. A central message of the Buddha is this: *Wake up!* To be awake and aware is the path to a new life that is happier, more joyous, and more enriching.

AWARENESS

RECOGNIZING BAGS OF GOLD IN OUR LIVES.

Compared to what we ought to be,
we are half awake.

—WILLIAM JAMES

Shiva and Shakti are the divine couple in Hinduism. *Shiva* means "the kind one, the friendly one," while the name *Shakti*, the female deity, means "force, power, energy." These two are among the most popular of gods and goddesses in the East. One day Shiva and Shakti are watching over the earth from the heavens. Both of them are deeply affected by what they see: the complexity of relationships, the challenges that face humans, and the ever-present and pervasive suffering around the globe.

As they watch, Shakti sees a miserably poor man walking down the road. His clothing has long since come apart at the seams, and his sandals are tied to his feet with an old rope. Shakti's heart is filled with compassion. She senses that the poor man is good but struggling, so she turns to her divine husband, Shiva, and begs him to give the man some gold. Shiva looks at the man for a long moment and thinks about his wife's request.

"My dearest wife," he says, "I cannot do that." Shakti, knowing Shiva to be friendly and kind, as well as all-powerful, is astounded. "What do you mean,

Husband? You are Lord of the Universe. Why can't you do the simple and compassionate thing of giving this man some gold?" Shiva responds, "I can't give this to him because he is not yet ready to receive it."

Now Shakti becomes angry, saying, "Do you mean to say that you cannot drop a bag of gold in his path?"

"I most certainly can," Shiva says.

"Then, please, Husband," Shakti pleads.

Immediately Shiva drops a bag of gold in the man's path. The man, however, is walking along thinking to himself, "I wonder if I will find food for this evening or will I go hungry again?" Turning at a bend in the road, he sees something on the path in his way. "Aha," he says. "Look there, a large bag of rocks. How fortunate that I have seen it. I might have torn these poor sandals of mine even further." Carefully stepping over the bag of gold, he goes on his way.

Life frequently drops bags of gold into our lives, but too often we are like the man in this story. Unable or unwilling to recognize it, we simply step over the gold and continue on. If we are wise, we will discipline our eyes and our minds to recognize those bags of gold, understanding that they rarely look like what they are. For many people, bad news is just that: bad news. For the wise among us, however, bad news can be something more, something that brings unexpected insights, new awareness, greater knowledge, a richer life path. Consider a young woman in her early twenties who was diagnosed with a deadly cancer. Until she had that "bad news" to deal with, the woman candidly says she was a perfectionist. Now, cancer has taken the edge off her driving perfectionism. Until she received the "bad news," she lived oblivious to others who suffered with life-threatening illnesses. Now, she works with an organization that raises money for cancer research. She and her supporters have raised nearly $100,000 to date. Her cancer is now in remission but of that "bad news" she says, "My life with cancer is better than my life without it."

In order to recognize our bags of gold, we need to be aware, awake and alert to life's many possibilities. Today, do a quick review of your life across the past few weeks, months, or even years. What's your bag of gold? Where did you encounter your bag of gold? What did you do? Did you recognize and receive it or did you step over it?

# BREATH

Don't just stand there, breathe!

> *Just as lions, elephants and tigers are gradually*
> *controlled, so the prana (breath) is controlled*
> *through practice . . . By proper practice of*
> *pranayama [breathing] all diseases are eradicated.*
> *Through improper practice all diseases can arise.*
> —SWAMI SVATMARAMA

The quote from Swami Svatmarama reveals the tremendous emphasis that Eastern sages place upon proper breathing. That same emphasis is stressed in the following story, in which the tongue, eye, ear, mind, and breath were caught up in an argument over which among them was the most important to the life of the body. Unable to resolve their debate, they appealed their creator, asking, "Who is the best of us?" The creator offered a simple way to decide: "The one whose departure makes the body seem worse is the best among you."

So, Tongue abandoned the body for a year, and upon returning asked, "How have you been able to live without me?" The others replied, "Like mute people, merely not speaking, yet we were able to see, hear, think, and breathe just fine!" Clearly, Tongue was not the best among them.

Next, Eye abandoned the body for a year, and upon returning asked, "How have you been able to live without me?" The others replied, "Like blind people, not seeing, yet we were able to talk, hear, think, and breathe just fine!" Clearly, Eye was not the best among them.

Then Ear abandoned the body for a year, and upon returning asked, "How have you been able to live without me?" The others replied, "Like deaf people, not hearing, yet we were able to talk, see, think, and breathe just fine!" Clearly, Ear was not the best among them.

Next, Mind abandoned the body for a year, and upon returning asked, "How have you been able to live without me?" The others replied, "Like children whose mind is not yet fully formed, yet we were able to talk, see, hear, and breathe just fine." Clearly, Mind was not the best.

Finally, Breath got ready to go and as Breath began to exit the body, all of the others realized immediately they could not live without Breath. "Breath," they cried out in unison, "you are the best among us. Do not leave us."

Those who seek to practice meditation are always instructed to begin by focusing on their breathing. In meditation, the breath is the vehicle of release: the releasing of distracting thoughts, disturbing images, feelings of limitation, and feelings of resistance. Those skilled in meditation know that the breath can calm, reassure, and stabilize both mind and body. You can prove this yourself with a simple practice. The next time you are feeling tense, anxious, or highly worried, simply remind yourself to take a deep breath. Almost always, the immediate effect is calming and stress-reducing. That's because when we are fearful, anxious, or angry, our breathing becomes irregular, adding to the tension. Interestingly, while the normal rate of breathing is around sixteen breaths per minute, the meditating sages often breathe only two or three times in a minute.

So the next time you're upset about something, don't just stand there, breathe! Here's an effective way of using the breath to calm and center yourself: While inhaling and exhaling, say to yourself: "Peace in, anxiety out." Repeat this as many times as necessary until calm and relaxation emerge.

BUDDHA

THERE'S A BUDDHA IN YOUR MIRROR!

We all have immense spiritual intelligence.

—VICTOR M. PARACHIN

For those of us who live in the West and who have been shaped largely by the European intellectual tradition, a good way to understand Buddha is through a comparison between Martin Luther and the Buddha. European history and Christianity itself were completely transformed when a monk named Martin Luther proposed alternatives to the Catholicism of his day. At the time, Catholic Christianity was largely a religion of rituals. with an elite priesthood ruling over a complex theology. Luther was regarded as radical because he advocated individual effort, plain language, and a simple approach to life and faith.

Buddha acted in much the same way. Buddhism arose in northern India around 500 BCE in response to complex Hinduism. Like the Catholicism of Luther's day, Hinduism was a religion of rituals, an elite priesthood, a complex theology, many gods, and a caste system whereby people were rigidly divided and severely restricted to predetermined roles. Like Luther, Buddha stressed the importance of individual effort and direct personal experience, rather than relying on a priest to be an intermediary.

This remarkable person known as Buddha (his original name was Siddhartha Gautama) was an immensely likeable and attractive individual. Unlike other spiritual leaders who claim to receive their wisdom as direct revelations from God, Buddha was rather ordinary. Basically, he said: "I'm a regular person who, through considerable struggle, managed to become enlightened." By "enlightened," he simply meant he understood suffering and how it could be ended. In various ways, he also told those around him, "If I can do this, anyone can."

Furthermore, he was clearly non-dogmatic. Buddha told his followers: "Try this for yourself" and "Don't believe it just because a teacher said so." On one occasion, he said: "Believe nothing, no matter where you read it, or who said it, no matter if I have said it, unless it agrees with your own reason and your own common sense." Contrast that gentle, confident approach with that of some religions, which pressure followers to embrace doctrines that defy the rational mind and are unbelievable. On another occasion, the Buddha taught: "Believe nothing merely because you have been told it. Do not believe what your teacher tells you merely out of respect for the teacher. But whatsoever, after due examination and analysis, you find to be kind, conducive to the good, the benefit, the welfare of all beings—that doctrine believe and cling to, and take it as your guide."

Here's a brief biography of Siddhartha Gautama. He was born in the sixth century BCE, the son of a wealthy ruler of a small kingdom. Gautama enjoyed a most privileged life, married, and became a father. In his twenty-ninth year, he managed to venture outside the palace and beyond the protection of royal advisors, where, for the first time, he saw the painful, harsh side of life: poverty, illness, aging, and death. What he saw shocked and transformed his life. Gautama reacted radically to his privileged lifestyle, abandoning it completely. He became a wandering holy man in pursuit of liberation and enlightenment. He radically transformed his lifestyle, embracing deprivation and asceticism. Eventually, Gautama realized that neither his life of luxury nor his life of asceticism was helpful, so he advocated a middle way between deprivation and indulgence. The key to a balanced life is moderation.

Still, after years of spiritual searching, the progress he wanted remained elusive. Desperate, Gautama decided to sit on a straw mat beneath a Bodhi tree, vowing to meditate and not move until he gained the insight he was seeking. After seven days, he opened his eyes because he understood how human suffering could be ended. This was his "enlightenment." The message he taught is condensed in the Four Noble Truths:

1. **Life is suffering.** To be human is to experience pain.
2. **Suffering has a cause.** All suffering is rooted in craving and attachment.
3. **Craving and attachment can be overcome.** When that is done, suffering ceases.
4. **The way to overcome craving and attachment is the Eightfold Path:**
    Right understanding
    Right purpose
    Right speech
    Right action
    Right livelihood
    Right effort
    Right mindfulness
    Right concentration

(In the chapter on "Possessions," we'll see how remarkably practical the Eightfold Path can be when applied to daily life.)

All schools and sects of Buddhism adhere to the Four Noble Truths and the Eightfold Path. However, after the Buddha died, his highly flexible and innovative philosophy came to be defined and taught more rigidly. As Buddhism spread, various cultures added their own unique symbols, prayers, rituals, temples, and myths. In some countries Buddhism was blended with pre-existing religions and philosophies. Japan, for example, tends to combine aspects of Shinto with Buddhism, while China adapted Buddhism to Taoist and Confucian thought. Consequently, there are now scores of different Buddhist paths. Some of the dominant Buddhist groups include Zen, Pure Land, Tibetan, Theravada, and Nichiren. In spite of the differences, varying Buddhist traditions tend to respect one another, avoiding labeling one as "right" and another as "wrong." Leading Buddhist teachers agree that Buddhism is a flexible religious philosophy that easily adapts to different cultures and times. It is worth nothing that there has never been a Buddhist war in which one Buddhist group attacks another because of conflicting beliefs.

One truly inspiring aspect of all Buddhist paths is the Buddha's immense confidence in us all. He emphasized over and over that like himself, each one of us can experience enlightenment, which is boundless wisdom and infinite compassion. Every time you look into a mirror, let your reflection remind you of this powerful truth: *There's a Buddha in my mirror!*

CHAKRAS

HARNESSING THE ENERGY WITHIN.

Chakras operate like interconnected,
self-opening valves that channel the
"electrical current" of the Universal Life Force
into the body.

—LIZ SIMPSON

Here's an experience most people have had. You meet someone for the first time and are instantly drawn to them. You find the person interesting, fascinating, pleasant, and naturally comfortable to be with. In their presence, you are instantly relaxed. On the other hand, there have been times when you meet a person and are instinctively put off by the individual. For reasons you can't immediately articulate, you find him or her boring, unpleasant, perhaps obnoxious and even offensive. It's a person with whom you can't establish a comfort zone. Eastern tradition explains that we all have those experiences because all living things are filled with energy, and all living things experience that energy in one way or another, knowingly or unknowingly. Our auras, or chakras, are interacting with the auras, or chakras, of others.

In Sanskrit, *chakra* means "wheel" or "disk." Eastern sages teach that chakras are vital energy centers flowing through the nerves up and down the spinal column and up to the head. Think of a vortex, which is a spiraling, whirling mass of water or air that sucks everything near it toward its center. Chakras are often described as spinning vortices channeling cosmic energy. These energies are considered part of our connection with the divine or higher consciousness. When the chakras operate optimally—that is, when we are most united with the divine—we experience physical, emotional, and spiritual well-being. On the other hand, when that energy is blocked or interrupted—when we are less connected to the divine energy—the result is confusion, emotional difficulty, and illness. There are seven chakras, and many ways to understand and interpret the chakra philosophy. Here's one that I find helpful. Look them over carefully and evaluate yourself and your lifestyle.

First chakra: The root or base chakra is located at the base of the spine. This chakra is focused on basic survival needs—breathing, shelter, safety, the health of our physical body. This chakra is out of balance in people who place too much emphasis on material wealth, status, or possessions.

Second chakra: The belly or spleen chakra is located in the lower abdomen and controls creativity—artistic, intellectual, and physical, as in our sexual energy. When it is free and unblocked, people experience passion and enthusiasm for living. Those who have an unbalanced and excessive belly chakra may be overly focused on satisfying desires. They are often people who struggle with addictive behavior. If this chakra is depleted, people deprive themselves of pleasure or believe they don't have what it takes to be successful, creative, and energetic.

Third chakra: The navel or solar plexus chakra is the center of our emotional life. It drives our self-esteem and self-confidence. When this chakra is in balance, people can act on their convictions and move forward in spite of resistance and criticism. They are not dependent on the approval of others. When it's out of balance, a person can be overly sensitive to the reactions of others, be easily discouraged, and unable to maintain a course of action.

Fourth chakra: The heart chakra is concerned with self-acceptance and matters of unconditional love. A person with healthy heart chakra is compassionate, kind, loving, and willing and able to reach out to others who are suffering. This individual has a great awareness of the interconnectedness of all beings. Those whose heart chakra is out of balance are unable to express affection and love easily; they are indifferent and don't exhibit much compassion for others.

Fifth chakra: The throat chakra controls creativity, self-expression, and communication, both verbal and nonverbal. People with healthy throat chakra are intuitive, often picking up on the thoughts of others before they speak. They can "read" people quite accurately. They are viewed as thoughtful, reflective people with great personal integrity. They communicate their feelings, thoughts, and needs without bombarding or overwhelming others. People whose throat chakra is unhealthy or out of balance can be overly talkative. They are energy depleters, and others don't like to be around them.

Sixth chakra: Often called the "third eye" chakra, it is located just above the eyebrows. This one deals with imagination and intuition. A person with a strong sixth chakra knows that intuition is a valid source of information, and combines it with other external sources of information to make wise decisions. People whose sixth chakra is highly developed often have extrasensory perception and telepathic abilities. Visualization is a power they easily and naturally tap into. When the sixth chakra is off-balance, however, a person will be overly stimulated and influenced by the psychic realm. Stereotypically, this person is "new age," "flaky," and easily caught up in the latest psychic rage.

Seventh chakra: The crown chakra is at the top of the head and deals with self-realization and inner knowledge. It is regarded as the key link between the human and the divine, and is the place from which our spirituality emerges. This chakra brings about a high level of consciousness. The great mystics and healers, found in every religious tradition, are people whose seventh chakra is highly developed. Those whose crown chakra is underdeveloped live a spiritually limited existence. They have little or no appreciation for the cultivation of a spiritual life. An imbalance in this chakra can be seen in people who are driven to amass material wealth or build a sense of personal power—common characteristics of the world's dictators.

In addition, each of the chakras also relates to specific parts of the body. Eastern medicine often works with chakras for healing physical problems people are experiencing. One way to harness the energy of chakras for yourself is to meditate on a problem area of your life or an issue that confronts you. Set aside some quiet time for meditation and reflection to gain insight as to why this area of your life or body is out of balance.

CHANGE

CHANGE YOURSELF AND YOU MAY CHANGE YOUR WORLD.

Everyone thinks of changing the world,
but no one thinks of changing himself.

—LEO TOLSTOY

Two men who wanted to gain greater spiritual truth learned that at the top of a nearby mountain lived a renowned spiritual teacher. After a very long and difficult climb up the mountain, they found themselves in the presence of the spiritual master. Bowing humbly, they asked the question which had driven them to the teacher:

"Master, how do we become wise?"

The teacher, who was in meditation, did not answer immediately. Finally, after a lengthy pause, he responded: "By making good choices."

"But teacher, how do we make good choices?" they asked almost in unison.

"From experience," said the teacher.

"And how do we get experience?" they asked.

"Bad choices," said the smiling spiritual master.

The spiritual master was not toying with the two spiritual seekers. He was encouraging them to practice regular, routine self-reflection. Critical reflection on our own thoughts, words, and behaviors is vital for spiritual and emotional growth. That man, who lived and meditated on the mountain, knew how important it was for people to practice self-inquiry. Such self-inquiry, to be most beneficial, must be done in a systematic way. Many spiritual teachers recommend a daily time of recollection and reflection whereby we calmly review our living. The goals of this practice are:

>to learn, not blame;
>to gain insight, not develop guilt;
>to be understanding, not condemning;
>to accept, not judge;
>to maximize strength while minimizing weakness.

This type of regular examination of conscience and spirit helps us to see where we need to make a change or take a corrective step. Doing so will bring about good choices, which in turn lead to good experiences. Another pleasant result is this: when we change ourselves, we often change our world.

COMPASSION

Practicing compassion to all living beings.

Every creature is full of God and is a book about God.

—Meister Eckhart

When we in the West talk about acting compassionately, most people automatically assume that this means compassion toward other people. However, in the East there is an enormous emphasis on the importance of practicing compassion toward all living beings, including animals and even the smallest of insects. Many stories are told to convey that virtue.

One story begins with Ganesh, the elephant-headed god, playing in a garden. Nearby in the house, his mother, the goddess Parvati, was preparing dinner. Out of boredom, Ganesh picked up a little kitten, playing with it rather roughly. She did not enjoy the rough play and hissed at Ganesh, hoping he would stop. He didn't listen, but rather continued bouncing, shaking, and finally dropping the kitten, leaving her with a scratch on her face.

Ganesh then went inside to see his mother and was shocked to see fresh blood on her face.

"Mother, who did that to you?" he asked, filled with rage. "I will teach them a lesson they won't forget. No one can hurt you. I won't permit it!"

"But, son, you gave me this scratch," she explained gently.

"No, I didn't. I would never hurt you."

"You did not know you were hurting me, my child. But when you scratched that little kitten, my face was scratched. Whenever you hurt any part of nature, you harm me and all of nature as well. Be more careful, my son."

That story is intended to teach the importance of nonviolence and compassion toward all living creatures. It's a lesson that Western cultures need to heed, as animal cruelty continues to be an enormous issue. Spiritual wisdom from the East reminds us that animals—including insects—are not merely other creatures with whom humans happen to share the planet. They are our companions and teachers and exhibit qualities that humans would do well to imitate. Like humans, animals have a complete repertoire of emotions, such as joy, fear, guilt, anger, contentment, embarrassment, gratitude, and grief. Many times they exhibit a loyalty that puts human conduct to shame. The East reminds us to honor all beings! Albert Schweitzer, the famed Christian physician, missionary, and Nobel Prize winner, did just that. He explained: "As a small child, I could not understand why I should pray for human beings only. When my mother first had kissed me good night, I used to add a silent prayer that I had composed for all creatures."

CONTROL

CONTROLLING THE MIND.

No enemy can harm one so much as one's own thoughts of craving, thoughts of hate, thoughts of jealousy and so on.

—THE BUDDHA

This story from the Native American tradition is remarkably Eastern in its lesson. A five-year-old boy is sent to spend the summer with his grandfather, who is a highly respected tribal elder. The boy adores his grandfather, observing his every move. After a few days, the boy notices a pattern in his grandfather's daily routine. Every morning at sunrise, his grandfather goes to a small altar in the corner of his home, takes off a necklace, and places it on the altar. Then he sits in silence for several minutes. Afterward, he puts the necklace back on and continues with his day. Every evening, at sunset, he repeats the same ritual.

Finally, the boy's curiosity prompts him to ask, "Grandfather, why do you do that every day?"

"I am taking some time to quiet my spirit and honor our ancestors," the elder replies.

"But what is on the necklace?" the boy asks.

The grandfather takes off the necklace and shows it to the boy. On it are the heads of two wolves.

"Grandfather, what do they mean?"

"Well," the grandfather explains, "inside each of us there are two wolves fighting to control us. One of them is scared and mean, and has a hunger that can never be filled. It cares only about itself. The other is brave and kind, and shares whatever it has with others. It cares as much about the community as it does for itself."

Wide-eyed and intrigued, the boy asks one more question: "Grandfather, which wolf will win?"

The elder smiles at his grandson, replying, "Whichever one we feed the most."

Of course, the lesson in that story is this: We have a responsibility to control the mind. When the mind is focused on right thoughts, right actions, right words, right effort, and right understanding, its impact can be enormous. The opposite is equally true. A focus on evil, greed, jealousy, and self-interest can have a horrific impact. Like the tribal elder, we all need to make time to quiet the mind and place our focus on healthy, wholesome thoughts.

We can control the mind. We can think positively. We can seek to see the best, not the worst, in others.

CONVERSION

The need for awareness versus conversion.

> *A human being is a part of a whole . . . He experiences himself, his thoughts and feelings, as something separated from the rest . . . a kind of optical delusion of his consciousness. This delusion is a kind of prison for us . . . Our task must be to free ourselves from this prison by widening our circle of compassion to embrace all living creatures.*
> —Albert Einstein

Many Westerners find it refreshing that Eastern religions are very laid back about conversion. Unlike Christianity and Islam, which are aggressive in attempts to convert people to their faith, the religions of the East are far less concerned about this. They feel no moral mandate to promote or force their faith views upon others. Eastern attitudes toward conversion or evangelization can be summed up in these points:

- Most Eastern spiritual leaders would not be in favor of conversion from one faith to another.
- Neither would they believe in the fusion of all religions into one. Eastern spiritual leaders compare the diversity of faiths to the beauty of the earth's

many flowers. For them, the world would lose much of its beauty if all flowers were blended into one.

- Ultimate Truth is one, but has an infinite number of aspects.
- All religions, though differing in philosophy and theology, are on a path that leads to the same goal.
- Eastern spiritual leaders have respect for all religions, because each one offers its own unique markers on the road to Ultimate Reality.
- The Infinite cannot be completely contained within any finite concepts.
- One single form of religion could not possibly satisfy everyone.

Of course, Eastern religions recognize that if a person of another faith wants to embrace Hinduism or Buddhism, that person has a full right to do so. However, Eastern spiritual leaders, teachers, and gurus would do a "reality check" to be certain that the person is doing so on the basis of reason and intellect. They would seek to clarify any misconceptions and be absolutely certain that the person is acting from their own inner wisdom and that the conversion is not due to external pressure or seen as an escape mechanism from their problems.

What Eastern spiritual leaders do believe in, however, is creating awareness. Their teaching and their practices are carefully designed to help people become more aware of their goodness and greatness; to help people recognize that the divine resides within each individual. The East would readily agree with Albert Einstein's observation that "our task must be to free ourselves from this prison by widening our circle of compassion to embrace all living creatures."

CRITICISM

CURBING CRITICISM.

The more one judges, the less one loves.

—HONORE DE BALZAC

A lmost all of us need to work at broadening our mercy and narrowing our criticism. We need to tone down the tendency to view and speak about others critically. Even Christians sometimes forget that Jesus warned his followers to banish critical and judgmental attitudes from their lives. "Stop judging others," he said simply and succinctly in the Gospel of Matthew (7:1). A critical, judgmental spirit is the opposite of a spirit characterized by love and acceptance. Those who have not learned to curb criticism and suspend judgment create a negative, hostile, and anxious spiritual atmosphere. Consider the lesson in this story about a Hindu, a rabbi, and a critic. While traveling separately through the countryside one afternoon, they were caught in an enormous thunderstorm. They each sought shelter at a nearby farmhouse.

"The storm will be raging for hours," the farmer told the three. "You should plan to stay here through the night. The problem is, there's only room enough for two of you. One of you will have to sleep in the barn."

Immediately the Hindu volunteered to be the one. "A little hardship is nothing to me," he said as he made his way to the barn.

A few minutes later there was a knock on the door. It was the Hindu who apologized, and explained, "There is a cow in the barn. According to my religion, cows are sacred, and one must not intrude into their space."

This time, the rabbi quickly stepped forward, saying, "Come in. Make yourself comfortable in the house. I will be happy to sleep in the barn." However, a few minutes later the rabbi returned to the house, saying, "I hate to cause a problem, but there is a pig in the barn. In my religion, pigs are considered unclean. I wouldn't feel comfortable sharing my sleeping quarters with a pig."

Finally, the critic said: "Oh, all right. I'll go sleep in the barn." He quickly made his way there. A few minutes later, there was a knock at the farmhouse door. It was the cow and the pig.

That story verifies the truth of this statement by Honore De Balzac (1799-1850): "The more one judges, the less one loves." Maintaining a vibrant, attractive, and compelling spiritual life means loving more and criticizing much less.

Consider taking on this challenge: Make a commitment that you will not criticize or judge anyone or anything for an entire twenty-four-hour period. When that period of time is over, look back and analyze it. Was it difficult? Were there many moments when you had to hold back? Did it make a difference in your life?

43

𝒟 DIVINITY

DISCOVERING THE DIVINITY WITHIN.

The kingdom of God is within you.

—LUKE 17:21

One day God grew weary of people and their incessant tirades and demands. So God told the angels, "I need to get away and hide for a while." God asked the heavenly advisors, "Where should I go? Where is the best place for me to hide out?"

Some said, "Hide on the highest mountain peak on the earth. They can't reach you there."

Others said, "No, hide at the bottom of the sea. They'd never find you there."

Then God turned to another angel, one known for great wisdom, and asked, "And where do you advise me to hide?" The angel thought for a moment and responded, "Go hide yourself in the human heart. That's the only place where they never go."

That Eastern concept of the God within each of us matches with the Western Christian concept articulated by Jesus, who said: "The kingdom of God is within you." The story about God and the angels, as well as Jesus' statement in Luke, are both reminders that each one of us must work at connecting with our higher self, the divine entity that dwells within each one of us. Most people experience moments when they are in touch with their higher self. Usually those experiences are connected with descriptions such as these:

I'm feeling on top of the world.
I'm feeling powerful, strong, in control.
I'm feeling extremely kind, compassionate, loving toward all beings.
I feel like I could move a mountain.

The goal is to have these fleeting, sporadic experiences with the higher self flow more regularly and routinely. A simple way to accomplish this is through the practice of meditation. A meditation for empowering this awareness of the higher self does not need to be a lengthy one. Even a few minutes of daily meditation begins to access this awareness, bringing it to the forefront of our living. Here is a basic meditation for greater spiritual development and awareness:

1. Sit upright in a comfortable position, either on a cushion or in a chair.
2. Breathe in and out to a count of forty complete breaths.
3. As you do this, try to relax completely, releasing tension of body or mind.
4. Continue to breathe and relax more deeply.
5. Contemplate your own divine nature. See it as a small light or small flame that you can fan and grow by exercising patience, love, and compassion for yourself.
6. Visualize that light growing larger, stronger, and more radiant, extending out of you, embracing and blessing everything and everyone around you.

7. Speak these affirmations silently and gently to yourself: *I am filled with divine light and energy. Divine love and light flow from me toward all around me. Divine love guides and leads me. Because of the divinity within me, I am a powerful, loving, compassionate, creative being.* Feel free to add your own unique affirmations.

8. Conclude by sitting quietly and again breathe in and out for forty complete breaths.

EMOTIONS

ARE YOU THE DRIVER OR THE DRIVEN?

> *There are those who discover they can leave behind*
> *destructive reactions and become patient as the earth,*
> *unmoved by the fires of anger or fear, unshaken as a*
> *pillar, unperturbed as a clear and quiet pool.*
>
> —THE DHAMMAPADA

A Japanese samurai warrior visited a Zen master, seeking answers to questions that had plagued him for some time.

"What is it you want to know?" asked the Zen master.

"Tell me, sir, do heaven and hell exist?"

"Ha!" laughed the Zen master in a contemptuous tone. "What makes you think you could understand such things? You are only an uneducated, brutish soldier. Don't waste my time with your ridiculous questions."

The samurai warrior froze in shock. No one spoke to a samurai that way. It meant instant death. Increasing the tension, the Zen master went on, "Are you too stupid to understand what I just said? Stop wasting my time and get out of here!" he shouted.

The samurai exploded with rage. As quick as lightning, his hand grabbed the sword, sweeping it over his head to get ready for the kill. In the split second before the sword descended to cut off the Zen master's head, the samurai heard him say, "This is the gate to hell."

Again, the samurai froze in astonishment. He got the message. It was his own rage that brought hell to him. The Zen master—as is customary among the greatest of Zen teachers—risked his life to make that fact inescapably clear. Pausing and then breathing deeply, the samurai replaced his sword. He bowed humbly, filled with respect and even awe.

"And this," smiled the Zen master, "is the gate to heaven."

This old story is all about moving out of emotional captivity. Many people are not the drivers of their emotions. They are driven by them; they are emotionally out of control. This is a significant personality weakness and a great danger. Uncontrolled anger and rage are major impediments to enlightenment. Buddhism compares untamed emotions to a forest fire that roars through a person, consuming all that is good, noble, and virtuous. In Christianity, anger is cited as one of the seven "deadly" sins. The Zen master is quite correct: an uncontrolled emotion is the gate to hell. The taming and directing of emotion is the gate to heaven.

The daily cultivation of attitudes such as gratitude, generosity, patience, kindness, compassion, and love can help us learn to manage our emotions, rather than be managed by them.

EMPATHY

THE TRANSFORMING POWER OF EMPATHY.

Bring your soul and interchange with mine.

—JOHANN FRIEDRICH VON SCHILLER

Once there was a prince who suffered from a mental illness. The man believed he was a rooster. To the dismay of his family and the royal court, he took off all his clothing, sat under a table, and refused to eat any food but corn seeds. His father, the king, sent for the best physicians and specialists in the land, but none of them could cure the prince of his delusion. Hearing about the prince's plight, a holy man from the kingdom appeared before the king, saying, "I think I can cure the prince." Desperate and with nothing to lose, the king gave him permission to try.

The wise man removed all his clothing, crawled under the table, and began to eat the corn seeds scattered around. The prince looked at him suspiciously and asked, "Who are you and what are you doing here?" The wise man answered, "Who are you and what are you doing here?" "I am a rooster," the prince said belligerently. Quietly, the holy man responded, "Really? So am I."

The two of them sat together under the table until they became accustomed to each other. When the holy man felt that the prince was comfortable with his

50

presence, he signaled for some clothing. He put on the clothes and then said to the prince, "Don't think that roosters can't wear clothing if they want to. A rooster can wear clothes and be a perfectly good rooster just the same." After giving some thought to those words, the prince agreed to put on his clothes.

Another time, the holy man signaled for food to be put under the table. At that the prince became agitated, shouting, "What are you doing?" "Don't be upset," the holy man reassured him. "A rooster can eat the food that human beings eat if he wants to, and still be a good rooster." Again, the prince considered this statement for a time and then he too signaled for food.

Then the holy man asked the prince, "Do you think that a rooster has to sit under the table all the time? A rooster can get up and walk around if he wants to, and still be a perfectly good rooster." The prince thought about that for a while, and then followed the wise man out from beneath the table and began to walk. After he began dressing like a person, eating like a person, and walking like a person, he gradually recovered his senses and began to live like a person.

The healing gift that the holy man brought to the king's son was empathy—the ability to feel and understand another person's pain. Empathy is one of the most valuable emotions we can cultivate. To be a person of empathy requires having both wisdom and courage. Unlike mere sentimentality, which is more about being nice, polite, and pleasing, empathy calls upon our deepest insights and strengths so that we can reach out to touch and transform those who are hurting. Change and healing can take place in the wounded only when they sense that we understand and feel their truth. Such is the power of empathy. Who in *your* social and professional circle is hurting today? What can *you* say or do that will make a difference?

*F*ORGIVENESS

PRACTICING THE FINE ART OF FORGIVENESS.

As we grow in wisdom, we pardon more freely.

—ANNE-LOUISE GERMAINE DE STAEL

This small footnote in history offers a large lesson in practicing the fine art of forgiveness. In 1922, Walter Rathenau, Germany's Jewish foreign minister, was assassinated by three German right-wing extremists. The men who committed this murder were motivated by political ideology and anti-Semitism. When the police captured them, two of them ended their lives by suicide. Only one of them survived to face trial, a man named Ernst Werner Techow.

Three days after the assassination, Mathilde Rathenau, the victim's mother, wrote to Techow's mother saying:

"In grief unspeakable, I give you my hand . . . Say to your son that, in the name and spirit of him he has murdered, I forgive, even as God may forgive, if before an earthly judge your son makes a full and frank confession of his guilt . . . and before a heavenly judge repents. Had he known my son, the noblest man earth bore, he would have rather turned the weapon on himself. May these words give peace to your soul."

Her words were read in open court and the public wondered if they would have any effect on the young assassin. Two decades later Techow would tell a Rathenau relative that the letter was his "most precious possession . . . it opened a new world to me." In prison he began to study seriously Jewish history and culture. He mastered Hebrew, becoming an erudite scholar of Judaism. In addition, Techow became highly sensitized to issues of anti-Semitism.

Sentenced to fifteen years, Techow was released from prison for good behavior after five years. In 1940, when France surrendered to Nazi Germany, Techow spotted an opportunity to repay Mathilde Rathenau's gracious act of forgiveness. He smuggled himself into Marseilles, where he began helping Jews to escape Nazi-dominated France. Techow was able to buy—or have forged—exit visas and permits allowing Jews to flee France for the safety of Spain. Always on the lookout for Jews he could help, Techow once asked a friend, "Do you know any Jews I could help to get out of here?" When the friend said he knew many, but that they had no money, Techow said: "Don't let that bother you. To be sure, those who are rich will have to pay a reasonable fee. But for every rich man I sponsor there are three penniless I help to escape for nothing."

In all, Techow helped over seven hundred Jews escape to Spain. No Jew who came to him was turned away. He provided the same service to those who were penniless and desperate as he did to those who could cover his expenses. Techow explained that his transformation and compassion toward Jewish people was set in motion by Mathilde Rathenau's letter: "Just as Frau Rathenau conquered herself when she wrote that letter of pardon, I have tried to master myself. I only wished I would get an opportunity to right the wrong I've done."

Forgiveness is a major theme in Judaism, Christianity, and Islam. It is also a highly regarded virtue in Eastern religious philosophy, and those spiritual teachers offer a variety of practices to develop a spirit of forgiveness. Eastern thinking understands that forgiveness is compassion in action. It has the power to uplift and transform our lives, and, sometimes, the lives of those whom we forgive. Forgiveness helps shed pain, bitterness, anger, and even hatred. Here is a six-step forgiveness meditation to practice when you are feeling wounded by someone else's words or deeds.

1. **Relaxation:** Use a quiet place where you won't be disturbed or distracted. Light a candle to symbolize the eternal light of divine love, compassion, and forgiveness. Sit comfortably on a cushion or a chair. Begin to relax your mind, spirit, emotions. Many find relaxation comes more easily when they focus on their breath. Simply breathe in and out, slowly and intentionally. Do this to a count of forty. Then meditate on the deity of your choice, asking for help in forgiving the person who hurt you.

2. **Recall** the person who hurt you and the words or actions that offended you. Without vilifying the person, simply focus on how you are feeling: angry, hurt, betrayed, bitter, furious, etc.

3. **Reframe** your experience by thinking of the other person. Understand that this person, like yourself, is changing every moment. Put yourself in his or her shoes. Try to see that they believed that their words or actions would give them pleasure or help them avoid suffering. Such motivations are often no different from our own.

4. **Respond** with forgiveness. Using the name of the person, say out loud: "I forgive you."

5. **Recognize** that you have made an intentional effort to forgive. Thank your deity or higher power for helping you with this effort.

6. **Repeat** this meditation as often as necessary and until you feel your forgiveness is complete. It often takes a series of forgiveness meditations to reach wholeness and peace.

GATHA

Taming the mind to become more focused.

*Our life is shaped by our mind; we become
what we think. Joy follows a pure thought
like a shadow that never leaves.*

—The Buddha

The word *gatha* refers to a short statement that can be recited during the day in order to better focus the mind for a specific activity. In Buddhist communities, a gatha is often a short verse from their sutras (scriptures). Interestingly, Christians often use a gatha, though it is not called that. For example, in order to focus positively on a new day, many Christians recite Psalm 118:24: "This is the day the Lord has made; let us rejoice and be glad in it."

However, a gatha does not need to come from a sacred scripture, though they often do. You can write your own to meet your own specific needs and situations. Its purpose is to encourage awareness, stimulate mindfulness, and generate focus and clarity. The key to a helpful gatha is brevity. Here are some examples of gathas:

- When feeling *anxious,* breathe in and say: "Calmness in." As you exhale, say: "Anxiety out." Repeat the phrase, combined with your breath, as many times as necessary: "Calmness in; anxiety out."
- When feeling *fear,* breathe in, saying: "Courage in." As you exhale, say:

"Fear out." Again, repeat as often as necessary until you feel less fearful and more courageous: "Courage in; fear out."

- When feeling *stressed,* follow the same pattern with your breath: "Peace in; stress out. Peace in; stress out . . ."

Unlike a mantra, which is always the same, gathas can be as different as the need or issue before you. Other ways to use gathas can include common daily events such as:

- *Eating:* "I am grateful for this meal and will consume it mindfully, appreciatively."
- *Exercising:* "I am grateful for the gift of my body. I will treat it with respect, giving it the activity it needs to remain healthy and strong."
- *Listening:* "My friend needs me to hear him/her. I remain open, receptive, and non-judgmental."
- *Working:* "My work allows me to feed, shelter, and clothe myself and my family. I am thankful and will offer my best on the job."
- *Driving:* "As I commute and drive, I do so with care and compassion for others on the road."

Consider developing your own gathas for your own specific needs. Let your creativity flow as you do this. You can also write gathas for a friend who is hurting or sick. For example, should you have a friend who is facing a life-threatening illness, you might offer your friend a gatha that could be used at the beginning of each day: "This new day is a precious gift. I have the opportunity to live this day in a way that will bring peace, joy, and contentment to myself and to everyone I encounter." Just remember that the purpose of a gatha is to help us become more aware of our thoughts and activities.

GENEROSITY

Cultivating a generous spirit.

A man there was, and they called him mad;
The more he gave, the more he had.
—John Bunyan

There were two monks who lived together for forty years. During those four decades they never once argued. Finally, one said to the other, "Don't you think it's time we had an argument, at least once?"

The other monk said, "Fine, let's start! What shall we argue about?"

"How about this piece of bread?" said the first monk.

"Okay, let's argue about this bread," agreed the second monk.

So, the first monk began the argument, saying, "This bread is mine; it belongs to me."

The second replied, "Oh, if it is, take it!"

Their argument never developed, most likely due to the fact that the second monk had spent a lifetime cultivating the habit of generosity. Eastern thought believes that life is governed by karma, a spiritual law of cause and effect. This principle holds that our actions in this life determine our rewards in the next life. (See the entry under "Karma" for further discussion.) Thus, it is important that we accrue good karma in this life by acting consistently with generosity and compassion.

Sometime today, close your eyes and take a few moments to consider how your actions impact your life and the lives of those around you. Ask yourself: *How would my life and the lives of those around me be different if I worked to be thoughtful, gentle, generous, kind, and compassionate at all times?*

GENEROSITY (Part 2)

BEING GENEROUS TO AN ENEMY OR ADVERSARY.

If you come across your enemy's ox
or donkey wandering off,
be sure to take it back to him.

—Exodus 23:4

A village in ancient India was being terrorized by a cobra whose attacks had resulted in the deaths of several people. Villagers tried unsuccessfully to capture the creature. Frustrated and desperate, they asked a holy man to intervene. The holy man was also a gentle man, in whose presence even wild animals felt comfortable and safe. So, in no time at all, he located the cobra and spoke to it: "You must not injure people anymore. This is not right. It is against the law of the gods."

The cobra was contrite, promising not to harm any more villagers. However, the next time the villagers spotted the cobra, they attacked it with sticks and stones, nearly beating it to death. The cobra crawled away and found the holy man, to whom it complained: "Look at me! Because of your advice I am nearly dead. How can that be the law of the gods?" The holy man replied, "I said you were not to bite people anymore. I never said you couldn't hiss to scare them away."

The holy man's answer is all about generosity to an enemy. He teaches us that we can and should stand up for ourselves, but that we should do so while taking care to cause the least possible trauma and trouble. For example, in any place of employment, there will always be someone who dislikes you, who refuses to help, who would prefer to see you fail than succeed. Rather than allow that person to turn you into a bitter cynic, or into someone who secretly harbors fantasies of revenge, the holy man's lesson is this: Try practicing generosity to your workplace adversary. You can offer your adversary the gift of making yourself as small a target as possible by:

- not making matters worse;
- respectfully listening to any complaints or criticisms your colleague may have about you;
- responding in a gentle, quiet tone;
- explaining yourself, your words and actions, without being defensive or angry; and
- maintaining ongoing integrity with your workplace adversary.

That's the lesson from the holy man and the cobra. That's also the meaning behind the words from the Jewish Bible: "If you come across your enemy's ox or donkey wandering off, be sure to take it back to him."

HAPPINESS

HAPPINESS IS SHAPED BY PERSPECTIVE.

Happiness is a matter of my attitude.
Happiness begins in the head.
—JOHN POWELL

There are many times in life when simply changing perspective on a situation can resolve the difficulty and unhappiness it presents. That is the point of this story about a villager who lived in a small one-room house with his wife, mother-in-law, six children, a cow, and six chickens. The cramped quarters were driving the man insane. Unhappy with his life, the man went to a rabbi who was known for his wisdom. "Rabbi," the man began, "I am going crazy, and will soon have a heart attack if things don't change. Please help me. I live in one room with my wife, her mother, six children, a cow, and some chickens." The rabbi thought carefully about the man's predicament and said, "I can help you solve your problem. Go out and buy a goat."

Overjoyed, the man promptly went out and purchased a goat. Now he had a wife, a mother-in-law, six children, a cow, a goat, and some chickens. His house was even more crowded and chaotic than ever. His unhappiness deepened so he went back to the rabbi and described the increased chaos. Once again the rabbi thought carefully about the man's predicament and said, "I can help you solve your problem. Sell the goat."

The man followed the elder's instructions and sold the goat. Suddenly, *all* he had in his small house were his wife, his mother-in-law, his six children, a cow, and some chickens. "I am so happy and positively peaceful without that goat," the man thought to himself happily.

If you're unhappy for any reason, reflect on that story. Perhaps, like the villager, you need to "sell the goat" in order to regain perspective. Happiness is shaped by our perspective. As you reflect, remember the wisdom in John Powell's words: "Happiness is a matter of my attitude. Happiness begins in the head." Sell the goat. Take whatever steps are necessary in order to gain a more balanced perspective. Remember the wisdom of this anonymous saying: "I complained bitterly because I had no shoes *until* I met a man who had no legs."

HUMILITY

THE IMPORTANCE OF HUMILITY FOR SPIRITUAL GROWTH.

Happy are the humble; they will receive . . .
—JESUS IN MATTHEW 5:5
(TODAY'S ENGLISH VERSION OF THE BIBLE)

A famous general was in an area where there lived a renowned Zen master. Since they were in close proximity, the general decided to visit the great Zen teacher. Arriving at the master's temple, the general presented his card, announcing himself to the temple secretary as "Anzai-san: Supreme Commander and General of the Imperial Army."

Taking the card, the secretary took it to the Zen master and returned. With considerable reluctance and trepidation, the secretary told the general: "The master said he has no business with you." Showing himself to be a man of some insight, the general took back his card, scratched off all the titles leaving only his name: Anzai-san. "Please take the card back to the master," he asked. On seeing the revised card, the Zen master responded: "Ah, Anzai-san. I would like to meet this man."

Humility is an important virtue in Eastern thought, just as it is in

Christianity. Leading the list of the "seven deadly sins" in Christianity is pride, or what we know as arrogance. Here are some reasons why humility is so vital for spiritual growth:

- With humility come sincerity and genuineness. When we are sincere and genuine, others are able to be equally open, sincere, and genuine. Honest dialogue can take place.
- With humility comes the openness to new truth, new insights, and new ideas. Without humility, learning cannot take place. The great Roman teacher Quintilian said this about some of his students: "They would no doubt be excellent students, if they were not already convinced of their own knowledge."
- With humility one realizes one's weaknesses, one's limits in knowledge and wisdom. Those who are humble are aware of their shortcomings and seek to remedy them.
- With humility comes a receptive spirit, a willingness to hear and learn. On the other hand, pride, arrogance, and vanity create a competitive spirit, which seeks to exhibit and promote one's own self. Lack of humility produces the narcissistic, self-absorbed individual. It's tough to be around people like that.
- With humility people are quick to listen and slow to speak. The arrogant and proud reverse that pattern, spouting their ideas and showing off their knowledge.

Let's go back to the story of the Zen master and the general. Unless the general had a proper sense of self, of humility, the Zen master knew he would simply be wasting his time with him. As long as the general was caught up in his own self-importance, there could be little significant conversation, dialogue, or learning. So, he instructed the secretary to tell the general, "I have no business with him." In the Zen tradition, those who lack humility are said to have about them the "stink of enlightenment." They believe they have arrived, and carry about themselves a sense of superiority and perfection. Prudently, the general immediately saw the error of his way and made a corrective move. Only then would the Zen master see him.

There are two lessons to be gleaned from the story of the Zen master and the general. First, humility is a prerequisite for all spiritual and emotional growth. Second, when pride and arrogance appear in a personality (and all of us have this tendency), a quick corrective can be made so that humility re-emerges. When humility is present, all other things are possible. That may be one reason why Jesus succinctly said: "Happy are the humble; they will receive . . ."

IDENTIFYING

IDENTIFYING THE SACRED IN EVERYDAY LIFE.

*Everything happening, great and small, is
a parable whereby God speaks to us, and the
art of life is to get the message.*

—MALCOLM MUGGERIDGE

One day God decided to become visible to a king and a peasant, and commissioned an angel to inform them of this blessed event. "O king," said the angel, "God has chosen to be revealed to you in whatever manner you wish. In what form do you want God to appear before you?"

Being pompous and arrogant because he had, for so long, been surrounded by awestruck advisors and subjects, the king said contemptuously, "How else would I wish to see God except in power and majesty? Show God to us in the fullness of power."

God granted the wish and appeared as a powerful, brilliant bolt of lightning, instantly pulverizing the king and his court. Nothing remained, not even a cinder. Everyone and everything was vaporized.

The same angel came to a peasant saying, "God wishes to be revealed to you in whatever manner you desire. How do you wish to see God?"

This puzzled the peasant. Scratching his head and pausing for a few moments, the peasant finally responded, "I am a poor man, not worthy to see God face to face. But if it is God's will and desire to be revealed to me, let it be in those things with which I am familiar. Let me see God in the earth I plow, in the water I drink, in the food I eat. Let me see God in the faces of my family, neighbors, and—if God deems it good for myself and others—even in my own reflection as well."

God granted the peasant his wish, and he lived a long, happy, healthy, holy life. Each of us would do well to emulate the peasant and seek to identify the divine presence permeating all of life—to see God in the grass and the flowers, in our pleasures and our pains, in those we love and in those we don't.

ILLUSIONS

Just deal with it.

Problems are only opportunities in work clothes.
—Henry J. Kaiser

An old farmer went to the Buddha seeking help for his problems. First, he had professional problems. In his part of the world, farming was extremely difficult and his work completely vulnerable to weather. "Either droughts or monsoons make farming too hard and unpredictable," he complained to the Buddha. "I can do all the plowing and planting, but the weather, which I cannot control, can ruin everything." Additionally, he had problems in his personal life. Even though he loved his wife, there were certain things about her he wanted to change. Similarly, he loved his children, but they weren't evolving the way he had hoped and anticipated. Listening carefully as the man explained his frustrations with life, the Buddha responded, "I'm sorry, but I can't help you."

"What do you mean?" questioned the farmer. "You're a highly regarded great teacher who has insight into all of life's problems."

"All human beings have eighty-three problems," the Buddha explained. "A few problems may go away, but soon enough others will arise. So we'll always have eighty-three problems."

The farmer, both indignant and frustrated, asked, "So what good is all of your teaching?"

To which the Buddha replied, "My teaching can't help with the eighty-three problems, but perhaps it can help with the eighty-fourth problem."

"What's that?" the farmer asked with great curiosity.

"The eighty-fourth problem is that we don't want to have any problems."

That last statement reveals the depth of the Buddha's insight into human nature. All of us have a deep-seated belief that life should be free of suffering. Think about how often these kinds of thoughts have entered your mind: *My marriage should be a happy and fulfilling one. My children should know better or be doing better. My supervisor is insensitive. My friend let me down. How could he do that to me? She should have known better. Why is this happening to me? What was he thinking when he said that to me? Life shouldn't be this hard. Life isn't fair.* Psychiatrists and psychologists actually have a name for this condition. Those who refuse to let go of resentments and hurts are engaging in "narcissistic entitlement." Left unchallenged, narcissistic entitlement can result in a person becoming bitter, angry, hostile, resentful, unwilling to forgive and unable to move on.

Oddly, the illusion that life should be free of suffering is often heightened in those who pursue spiritual practices, because they erroneously believe that all problems will disappear if one is "spiritual" enough. Thinking the right way, speaking the right way, acting the right way—none of these can provide immunity to problems, although these practices can prevent many issues and minimize the fallout. What spiritual practice can do is help us deal with those matters in a calmer, more balanced way. The Buddha is right: Because we live in an imperfect, messy world, we will always have "eighty-three" problems. Expecting not to have problems is one of our great illusions about life. If he were here today, the Buddha might very well say: "Get real. Wake up. Abandon the illusions about how life *should* be and face life as it *really* is."

This does not mean that we should wring our hands in despair but rather that we should simply and straightforwardly expect difficulties in our life's journey and face them with courage and detachment. This perspective can help also when we recognize that problems are always opportunities for us to gain new insights, new strengths, new ways of thinking and acting. Our greatest growth comes when we encounter and deal with life's challenges.

JUDGING

DON'T JUDGE TOO QUICKLY.

*The acceptable and the unacceptable
are both acceptable.*

—LAO TZU

A wise and prosperous farmer lived in northern China. He had the respect of all his neighbors because of the way he lived his life and the way he conducted his affairs. Following a violent storm in the area, he went out to his field one day and discovered that his best horse, a magnificent stallion, had been terrified by the storm and had broken free from the corral. The fine creature was nowhere to be found. The farmer's neighbors heard about the loss and came by that evening to express their sympathy, saying, "What bad luck." His neighbors were surprised when the farmer merely responded, "Who knows what is good luck and what is bad luck?"

The next day his stallion returned, bringing with him a herd of wild horses, all equally as strong and fast. Again, neighbors rushed over, but this time in a festive mood, saying, "What good luck." A second time the old farmer responded, "Who knows what is good luck and what is bad luck?"

A few days later the farmer's only son was riding one of the wild horses. The mare threw him high into the air and when he landed, his leg was broken in several places. The kind neighbors came by to check on the young man, and said to the father, "What bad luck." A third time the farmer replied, "Who knows what is good luck and what is bad luck?"

Later in the week, the army came through the village to inform the villagers that a border war was taking place. They conscripted all of the young men in the village into the army. Because the farmer's son had a broken leg, the army left him behind, saying he was an invalid. Again the neighbors came by, saying, "What good luck." But once more, the farmer responded, "Who knows what is good luck and what is bad luck?"

That story is instructive in two ways. First, it is a reminder that life is often a series of events oscillating between the ups and downs, between peaks and valleys, between easy times and hard times, between ecstasy and pain. When we truly realize that flow of life, we can be more patient with the down times, and like Lao Tzu, come to the place where we can say "the acceptable and the unacceptable are both acceptable." Second, that story powerfully teaches us that we should not be hasty in making judgments about what is good and what is bad. Often what initially appears as an enormous burden in our lives proves to be a significant blessing.

KARMA

CLEARING OUT NEGATIVE KARMA.

> *Love God and selflessly serve others.*
> *Your past evil karma will become like*
> *a cancelled check.*
>
> —MATA AMRITANANDAMAYI

Karma is a chain of cause and effect based on our mental and physical actions. It impacts life in the present and determines our destiny in a future life. Although this concept is strikingly Eastern, even Christianity alludes to it in several places. For example, the apostle Paul wrote: "Remember this: whoever sows sparingly will also reap sparingly, and whoever sows generously will also reap generously" (2 Cor. 9:6). In another place, he writes: "Do not be deceived . . . A man sows what he reaps . . . Let us not become weary in doing good, for at the proper time we will reap a harvest if we do not give up" (Gal. 6:7, 9). This law of action and reaction, cause and effect, is also cited by Jesus: "Give and it will be given to you" (Luke 6:38).

In the East, the process of reincarnation is driven by karma—we reap what we have sown. Karma is not about fate and fatalism, as some have presented it.

Rather karma is the understanding that we mold our lives much like a potter fashions a pot. The popular expressions "What goes around, comes around" and "You get what you give" both reflect this insight.

The good news is that we can redirect the flow of karma. This is important to understand, especially when our lives seem to be in disarray or are moving in unhealthy directions. Here are some methods that Eastern sages have long recommended for redirecting and clearing out the negative karma that we have developed and that is hurting us:

• **Worship.** Meditation, prayer, chanting, singing praises to God—all of these restore positive karma in life. If regular worship is not currently part of your life, you might consider joining with others at a temple, church, or synagogue, or you can set up a small worship table in a corner of your home or apartment.

• **Service.** Volunteer your time and talents on behalf of those who are in need. This kind of selfless service is highly regarded in Eastern thought and believed to be one of the most effective ways of defusing negative karma.

• **Charitable donations.** Give of your money to organizations working to improve the lives of others. You can connect your donation to events in your life. For example, if you've had a bout with cancer, raise and give money for cancer research. If you've been in an accident and the victim of a drunk driver, donate to a group seeking to reduce drunk driving incidents.

• **Pilgrimage.** Historically, people have made long and sometimes difficult journeys to sacred sites in order to worship and venerate the site, or in order to ask there for supernatural aid, or to discharge some religious obligation. If finances are an issue, it is not necessary to travel around the world to make a pilgrimage. You can accomplish the same goals by visiting a sacred site close to home, perhaps a historic church, synagogue, or temple, or any other location that attracts you spiritually.

• **Self-denial.** You can overcome various karmic consequences by voluntarily embracing austerity for a period of time. Some choose to do a fast day once a week. Others decide to do a silent weekend retreat twice a year. Still others deny themselves various luxuries such as a new car, new clothing, or a new home, even though they could easily afford them. The money not spent is donated to a worthy cause.

• **Devotion.** Connecting in a deep and personal way to a higher power also eases karmic sting. This devotion could be to the Virgin Mary, Jesus, a saint, or one of the many Eastern deities. Learn all you can about that deity; offer prayers of praise and adoration; ask for guidance and wisdom.

• **Mantra.** The intentional reciting of a mantra many times during the course of a day also offsets bad karma. A mantra is a set of words with a religious significance and power. It can be saying the Hail Mary, the Lord's Prayer, the Jesus Prayer ("Lord Jesus Christ, Son of God, have mercy on me, a sinner") or even just the sound *Om*. Find one that resonates with your spirit and use it frequently.

Basically, redirecting the negative effects of karma means being compassionate and generous as well as acting skillfully and wisely. Right thoughts and right actions ease the karmic burden.

KARMA (Part 2)

WHAT IS YOUR KARMIC COLOR?

> *Be always mindful of what you are doing and thinking.*
> *So that you may put the imprint of your immortality*
> *on every passing incident of your daily life.*
>
> —ABD'L KHALIQ GHIJDEWANI

Eastern philosophy, particularly that found in the Jain religious tradition, says that each of us comes into this world carrying a karma or burden that impedes us in our quest for liberation and freedom. By right thoughts and right actions, we are quite capable of eliminating those karmic restraints. Five colors are associated with the karma we carry. Here is a traditional story that illustrates how personality traits are connected with those five colors. Read the story carefully, asking yourself: *What is my color?*

A hungry person with the most negative *black* karma will uproot and kill an entire tree to obtain a few mangoes. The person of *blue* karma fells the tree by chopping the trunk, again merely to take a handful of fruits. A third person with *gray* karma spares the trunk, but cuts off the major limbs of the tree. The person with *orangeish-red* karma carelessly and needlessly lops off several branches to reach the mangoes. The fifth, exhibiting *white* (or virtuous) karma, simply approaches the mango tree and picks up the ripe fruit that has naturally dropped from the branches to the foot of the tree.

That story is worth examining more fully. The first three individuals are acting out of desperation. Hungry, they destroy limbs, trunk or even the entire tree to satisfy their need, without considering how harmful their actions are. The fourth person exhibits something of an ability to see beyond the immediate, but still is destructive in securing the mangoes. The first four have, in effect, declared war on the mango tree. What distinguishes the first four is merely the degree of destruction they cause in gathering the fruit. Their thinking leads them to discount the tree's value and permits them to destroy it in order to enjoy the fruit. They are not fully aware nor awake.

Only the fifth person is awake and aware and therefore demonstrates deeper ways of thinking and acting. He clearly sees beyond his own needs and is content to eat the fruit that has already fallen to the ground, leaving the tree to continue bearing mangoes so that others who come may also feed their hunger.

Today, conduct an examination of your soul by asking: *What is my color? Which of the five people am I most like?* Then, become more aware, alert, awake. Consider ways you can begin to develope daily practices that will lighten the color of your karma.

KINDNESS

UNITING THE WORLD THROUGH KINDNESS AND LOVE.

> *The effort of the genuine spiritual seeker*
> *should be to cultivate love until the mind*
> *becomes saturated by it.*
> —BHANTE Y. WIMALA

Ramana Maharshi (1879-1950) is regarded as one of the greatest spiritual teach-ers of modern-day India. At the young age of seventeen, Sri Ramana Maharshi experienced a powerful moment of enlightenment, without the guidance of a guru. Because of that experience, he left home without his parents' permission, making his way to the holy mountain of Arunachala in southern India. There he spent sever-al years in silence, first in a dark corner of a temple at the foot of the mountain, and later in various caves on the mountain itself. After several years of silent reclusion, he emerged, mainly because spiritual seekers were aware of him and had questions. Sri Ramana followed no particular teacher or teachings but spoke directly out of his own experience in responding to questions. Interestingly, he wrote nothing himself, but some of his question-and-answer sessions with seekers were transcribed by fol-

lowers. Before long, an ashram grew up around him, where he continued to teach and be visited by spiritual seekers from all over the world.

One of the most fascinating stories about this Indian yogi tells of his evening walks. As he left his ashram for his walk, cows from a neighboring village would break from their ropes, running to join him. Local dogs trotted alongside, and young children followed behind. The story adds that even wild animals would emerge from the jungle to accompany him, including various kinds of snakes. Hundreds of birds would fly low in the sky, hovering over the yogi and his companions, acting as flying squadrons providing protection. When he completed his walk and returned to his room, all of his companions disappeared.

The interpretation of that story is this: Ramana Maharshi was so filled with kindness and love that his very being emanated those qualities. Like a magnet, life gravitated instinctively toward him. Lest this story seem farfetched to a Western mind, it is worth noting that similar stories are told about the Christian Saint Francis, whose closest friends and frequent companions were animals and birds.

The example of this saintly yogi is, in the East, a reminder that growing such love and kindness is the objective of authentic spirituality. The teachers of the East remind us that every human being has this same potential as Ramana Maharshi and Francis; that their goodness is humanly attainable and readily within our reach. *If we so desire,* such love and kindness can become part of *our* daily living. Think about that today. Wherever you go, what is the energy that emanates from you? Is it impatience or patience? Is it intolerance or tolerance? Is it hostility or hospitality? Is it kindness and love, the kind that unites the world?

LESSONS

Teachers are everywhere.

Imagine that every person in the world is
enlightened but you. They are all your teachers,
each doing just the right things to help you learn
patience, perfect wisdom, perfect compassion.

—The Buddha

"When the student is ready, the teacher appears" is a very common phrase in Eastern thought. Many stories are told that illustrate this truth. One tells of a student who heard about a famous spiritual master living in the mountains. No one was sure exactly where the master lived, so the student searched far and wide. For a long time he was unable to find the elusive sage, but nonetheless continued his search.

After several years, he found the master's small hut deep in the forest. Inside was a small altar, a few scrolls, and some books that were so esoteric that the student could not begin to understand them. The only furnishings were a rough wooden table, small bed, a hearth, and a jar of water. The student waited and waited inside the hut, but no one came. For many, many months the student returned to the hut and waited, but no one was ever present. However, he remained hopeful, because sometimes the hearth was warm and at other times the scrolls had been moved.

Decades passed and the student became content to wander the mountain and forest trails. He spent much of his time in solitary meditation and reflection. One day, he came upon the hut and went inside. After only a few minutes, the master—now a very old sage—walked in. Immediately, the student fell to his knees, asking the master to accept him as a student. The teacher nodded, saying that it was obvious that the conditions were right for them to meet, and that he was accepting the student without further discussion or delay.

That story—and many others like it—conveys how important timing and learning are: "Only when the student is ready, does the teacher appear!" Too often, too many people miss the most important teachers of their lives simply because they are not ready, not open, not able to recognize the lessons that the teacher is present to bring them. The Buddha reminds people today that the best way to avoid missing out is to "imagine that every person in the world is enlightened but you. They are all your teachers, each doing just the right things to help you learn patience, perfect wisdom, perfect compassion."

LOVING-KINDNESS

BLESSING YOUR CORNER OF THE WORLD WITH LOVE.

> *Put away all hindrances, let your mind full of love pervade...the whole wide world, above, below, around and everywhere, altogether continue to pervade with love-filled thought, abounding, sublime, beyond measure.*
> —THE BUDDHA

In every authentic spiritual life there is the quality of loving-kindness. While this can arise naturally in some circumstances, such as the love of a parent for a child or a partner for a spouse, on most other occasions it must be intentionally cultivated. One ancient practice (it goes back at least twenty-five hundred years) is the loving-kindness meditation. It is easy to do and highly satisfying because it evokes friendliness and compassion toward oneself and toward others.

To begin, find a quiet place where you can repeat to yourself the simple words of this meditation. It can be done in your home, office, or car; in a park, on a playground; on buses or airplanes; in doctors' waiting rooms—anywhere you can sit comfortably and be quiet. If you're new to meditation practices, try doing this for a mere five minutes. If you've had a little more experience or have a little more time, try spending ten to twenty minutes on it. This loving-kindness meditation begins with yourself and then radiates outward. It is recommended that we start with the self because it is difficult to love others if we are unable to love ourselves.

Begin by placing the focus on yourself, and then repeat these four sentences:
May I be filled with loving-kindness.
May I be free of suffering.
May I be at peace.
May I be happy.
Repeat the four sentences, allowing their good intentions to sink deeply into your body and mind.

Then place the focus on someone you love:
May (name) be filled with loving-kindness.
May (name) be free of suffering.
May (name) be at peace.
May (name) be happy.
Again, repeat these so that you will evoke loving-kindness toward your loved one.

Next, offer this meditation for a friend or colleague:
May (name) be filled with loving-kindness.
May (name) be free of suffering.
May (name) be at peace.
May (name) be happy.

Repeat the four sentences to deepen loving-kindness attitudes toward this person.

On the next cycle, offer the meditation for a stranger, perhaps the man who makes your coffee at your favorite coffee shop, or the woman who rides the same bus as you do:

May he/she be filled with loving-kindness.

May he/she be free of suffering.

May he/she be at peace.

May he/she be happy.

As you continue to repeat these, you will begin to feel a sense of compassion toward these strangers who are part of your life.

Finally, if you really want to challenge yourself, offer the loving-kindness meditation for an enemy or some difficult person in your life. It may be someone who has treated you unkindly or even cruelly, or someone who betrayed your confidence. Perhaps it may be someone who has gossiped about you and hurt you deeply:

May (name) be filled with loving-kindness.

May (name) be free of suffering.

May (name) be at peace.

May (name) be happy.

Continue repeating until your feelings of anger, hurt, and disappointment begin to soften. Most people discover that this loving-kindness meditation is calming and enlarges the heart.

MEDITATION

THE IMPORTANCE OF CULTIVATING SILENCE IN DAILY LIFE.

*Meditating regularly helps you to access and release
the power of your innate peace, love, and joy.*
—MIKE GEORGE

In the West, people constantly search for ways to create or increase their personal happiness and inner peace and harmony. Often they seek to reach these goals by striving for increased wealth, power, education, or social status. An underlying assumption is that happiness will result from having fine things such as a large home or a luxury vehicle.

In the East, people have similar desires for happiness, inner peace, and harmony. The path to those goals, as identified across the centuries by sages, is meditation. While there may be nothing wrong with having wealth, power, education, or social status, a large home or a luxury vehicle, those things do not ultimately generate the inner calm and unity that people seek. The key to happiness lies in taming the mind, and that is done through the regular practice of meditation. Here are just some of the benefits of meditation:

- If you live a busy, hectic life, meditation can help you relax and release stress.
- If you are prone to worry and anxiety, meditation can restore inner calm.

• If you are a person facing major life issues, meditation can give you courage and strength to deal with them.

• If you are lacking in self-confidence and are often hesitant and uncertain, meditation can provide you with stability and confidence.

• If you are a fearful person, afraid to risk and branch out, meditation can provide you with insight into the real nature of your fears, freeing you to overcome the fear based in your mind.

• If you are dissatisfied with your life and feel everything you've done is meaningless, meditation can help you find a meaningful way to live.

• If you are wealthy, meditation can empower you to realize your blessings and help you see how to use your wealth for your happiness as well as for others.

• If you struggle financially, meditation can help you cultivate contentment and cut down on feelings of jealousy or resentment toward those who have more than you.

• If you have an addiction of any kind—to alcohol, drugs, tobacco, sex—meditation can give you the insight and strength to overcome these dangerous habits.

• If you tend to be a self-centered, self-absorbed person, meditation can provide you with a more realistic sense of self, making you a more pleasant person to be around, and helping you to take a sincere interest in others and their needs.

• If you are an angry, hostile, aggressive person, meditation can help you to understand why this is so and to transform that negative energy into positive forces such as patience, kindness, and compassion.

In addition to the benefits cited above, many scientific studies indicate that regular meditation is very good for the body as well as the mind. Physical benefits of meditation include decreased blood pressure, cholesterol levels, and heart rate; and even protection from brain deterioration.

Although the benefits of meditation are numerous and clear, many people feel the practice is beyond their level of skill and expertise. This is definitely not true. Meditation is actually quite easy. Here is a basic ten-minute meditation to get you started (you will also find other meditation exercises throughout this book):

• Find a quiet place where you can be without distractions.

• Sit on the edge of a chair, keeping your back straight, your pelvis slightly forward, your shoulders level, and your chin relaxed.

• Breathe normally, maintaining your posture. Relax any part of your body that is tense.

• Count your breath on each exhalation, counting out forty breaths. Various thoughts will enter your mind. Simply be aware of them, let them go, and return to counting your breath.

• After you have done this for a few minutes, move on to repeat a soothing phrase, perhaps a quality you need for the day: love, kindness, compassion, patience, peace, joy, etc. Some people find it helpful to focus on a deity, repeating the name: Jesus, Allah, Buddha, Mary, God, etc.

After you've done this once, you will be pleased with yourself. Then, try to meditate each day for ten minutes, gradually building up to longer sessions. The goal is to have a more settled and focused mind. One Tibetan lama explains that before he began meditating, his mind was like a stag with great antlers trying to make its way through a thick forest; the animal got snagged on branches time after time. But after many years of practice, his mind was more like a monkey in a jungle, swinging freely from vine to vine.

MIND

HAVING A SETTLED MIND.

> *The mind becomes settled when it cultivates friendliness in the face of happiness, compassion in the face of misery, joy in the face of virtue, and indifference in the face of error.*
> —PATANJALI

From the mid-tenth century through the seventeenth century a military class called the samurai was a vital part of Japanese life and culture. Samurai were bound by a strict code of honor called *bushido,* and were expected to set an example for those below them. So committed were they to their code of honor that a disgraced samurai could regain honor and respect only by committing suicide. There are many instructive stories of the samurai. One of them tells of a samurai who is being chased by a hungry bear. The samurai manages to outrun the bear, but in so doing, literally runs off a cliff. As he is falling downward, he grabs a branch. Clinging desperately, he looks up to see the bear leaning over the cliff clawing at his head, missing only by inches. As he looks down to the ground below, only about twelve feet, he sees a lion leaping up, missing his feet only by inches. As the samurai looks at the branch he is clutching, he sees two groundhogs gnawing away at it. His lifeline is disappearing before his very eyes, bite by bite. Taking a long, deep breath, the samurai notices, next to his branch, a clump of wild strawberries. In the midst of the clump is a large, plump, juicy strawberry. With his free hand, the samurai reaches over, picks the strawberry, puts it in his mouth, chews it slowly, and says, "Ah—delicious."

That story has been told and retold among the Japanese for centuries. It is popular because it stresses the importance of having a settled, focused mind. The samurai is in a situation over which he has no control. Despite his high-level warrior skills, the samurai cannot escape his predicament. Realizing that, he does four things:

1. He breathes deeply.
2. He remains calm.
3. He acknowledges the situation for what it is.
4. He takes advantage of the only opportunity that presents itself, the eating of the strawberry.

Behind his ability to remain so calm and collected is his capacity to practice acceptance. The samurai, understanding that there is no choice, chooses to accept rather than resist, lash back, or complain bitterly. For him, acceptance is not the same as giving up; it is a choice he makes. The samurai chooses to move beyond judging, beyond being angry, beyond feeling a sense of injustice. He simply, wisely, and maturely faces his reality: "It is what it is."

The attitude demonstrated by the samurai is one that all of us ought to strive for, especially when situations come our way that we cannot control or change. For example, we can be diagnosed with a life-threatening illness, our partner may no longer wish to remain with us, the company we work for can be bought out and our job eliminated, someone we love deeply could be killed by a drunk driver. The list

of traumas that can come tumbling into our lives is endless. Rather than complain and protest about life's injustices, we need to have a mind that is settled enough to accept the situation and face it directly. To fight it or deny it only results in additional stress for ourselves. The samurai teaches us that it is possible to face life's hardships without falling apart. By remaining composed, calm, cool, and collected in the face of our struggles, we have greater ability and energy to take advantage of whatever opportunities are present.

NAMASTE

RECOGNIZING AND RESPONDING TO THE DIVINE WITHIN.

> *The spirit is so near that you can't see it!*
> *But reach for it . . . Don't be the rider who gallops all night*
> *and never sees the horse that is beneath him.*
>
> —RUMI

When a yoga class concludes, it is common for the instructor to place her hands together in front of her chest, as if in prayer, and end the session by bowing and saying *Namaste*. The word is a greeting that means "I salute the divinity in you." Eastern teachers always remind people that the divine (or God) is present within each person. Throughout countries such as India and Nepal, people greet each other not with our "hello," but with the word *Namaste*: "I salute the God within you." Behind this greeting is the realization that our bodies are repositories of the divine. Our task on this earth is one of movement toward divinity, to become our true, divine self.

That is the point of this story in which a young man in search of God traveled to a distant country, where he sought out counsel from an elderly woman. Many considered her a saint. She lived simply in a small hut furnished with only the most basic necessities: a bed, a stove, some dishes and pots. As they sat together, the young man felt a soothing peace. After they had spent time in silence, he asked the question that burned in his heart: "Do you know where I can find God?" The woman studied his face for a moment and replied, "That's not an easy question. I need to think on it so I can answer you clearly. Can you come back tomorrow after I have had time to meditate?" The young man nodded his assent. As he left, the woman asked, "Would you bring me a glass of milk when you come?"

That night the man tossed and turned because he was most anxious to revisit the woman and hear her answer to his question— "Do you know where I can find God?" He returned to the hut, bringing the glass of milk as requested. She welcomed him in, and again they sat together for a few moments of silence. He waited, but was obviously impatient and eager to hear her response. Yet she did not speak, but poured the milk into her begging bowl. Then she began stirring it with her fingers as if she was looking for something inside the milk. The liquid simply ran through her fingers. She frowned as it fell back into the bowl. She did this over and over and over again.

This went on for some time, the woman stirring the milk and the young man quietly watching. Growing extremely impatient, the young man finally blurted out, "Please, what are you doing? What are you looking for?" This time she looked directly at the young man, saying, "I heard there was butter in milk. I'm looking for the butter, but can't seem to find it." The young man almost burst out laughing at what he believed to be her ignorance. Correcting her, he said, "No, no. It's not like that at all. You don't understand—the butter isn't in the milk. It's not separate from it. You have to convert it. You have to churn the milk to make the butter come out."

Now the woman beamed at him. "Very, very good! You do understand. And you have the answer to your question." But he didn't get it, so she elaborated, saying, "It is time for you to go home. Go and churn the milk of your life, of your heart and soul, of your relationships. There you will find God. Remember: keep stirring, lifting, swirling, converting, transforming. God's there: hidden in your life, not separate from it, or from you." Those who adhere to the Christian faith might be interested to know that Jesus offers the very same teaching. In the Gospel of Luke, Jesus declares to a rather surprised group of listeners: "The kingdom of God is within you" (Luke 17:21). Like the young man in the Eastern story, Jesus' audience sought God "out there," in all sorts of other places and spaces. Yet, the reality is that we carry the divine and all things connected to that divinity inside of us.

So, the next question is: *How do I tap into that inner divinity?* We can do this by recognizing and responding to our inner spiritual self, by speaking kindly, acting justly, showing mercy, loving unconditionally, and treating all beings with compassion and kindness. Aids in that process include meditation and prayer. Remember that we are all gods and goddesses walking on this planet for a brief period of time. Our task is to live out what we truly are.

NONATTACHMENT

Just let go!

Peace comes when grasping ceases.

—Victor M. Parachin

Eastern thought holds strongly to this basic principle: *Attachment leads to suffering. Nonattachment leads to freedom from suffering.* While that is a true and simple concept, its application is challenging. Consider the problem this woman created for herself. Writing to an advice columnist, she describes herself as a divorced mother dating a divorced man whose children are almost completely grown. Her boyfriend makes "significantly more" money than she does, and has the luxury of being able to take a great deal of time off from work for travel and to pursue his hobbies. "My problem is, I find myself feeling jealous and resentful of the opportunities he is fortunate to have. I know I shouldn't feel that way. He has earned his success and I want him to have all the things he enjoys." Unlike her boyfriend, this woman struggles to make ends meet. Her companion generously offers to give her money from time to time, an offer which she graciously declines. Yet, in the end, this woman says she still feels angry over his more fortunate style of life.

That woman's dilemma is the point of this famous Indian tale about the way to catch a monkey. You drop a handful of nuts into a jar with a small opening. The monkey comes and puts his hand into the jar, grabs the nuts, and then discovers that he can't get his fist out through the opening. If the monkey would just let go of the nuts, he could escape. But he won't. That is the woman's dilemma. She has her hands on the nuts inside a jar. To escape she must let go, detach, but she is unwilling and therefore remains captive to her feelings.

What the woman needs to practice—and this is true for all of us—is the Eastern art of nonattachment, sometimes referred to as detachment. Nonattachment is the emotional key that unlocks the doors of our soul, permitting us to walk away from suffering into contentment. So, today, you might want to ask yourself: "What am I holding on to?" "What is my fist clinging to inside the jar?" Then, challenge yourself to just let go. Keep in mind also that practicing nonattachment is a lifelong process. It is a commitment that must be renewed on a daily basis.

NONHARMING

Honoring all beings.

> *O God, enlarge within us the sense of fellowship with all*
> *living things, our brothers the animals to whom you gave*
> *the earth as their home in common with us...*

—Basil, the Great

Central to Eastern religious philosophy is the theme of nonharming. Behind that precept is a profound respect for all life, human and animal. Eastern spiritual teachers stress respect for all life and the honoring of all beings, including animals. As a result, vegetarianism is far more common in the East than here in the West. Consider the inspiring example of Chaitanya Mahaprabhu (1485-1534), an Indian scholar and mystic born in Bengal, who lived his life according to the principles of nonharming and nonviolence. He reportedly was instrumental in converting many cruel, unkind people, who became both compassionate and gentle. Anecdotes from his life indicate that he helped transform criminals and bandits into productive, kindhearted citizens.

One story indicating his influence tells of a time when he learned that hundreds of cows and bulls were being killed every year to feed the Muslim ruler of his area. The slaughter of innocent creatures saddened and disturbed Chaitanya, so he went to the court of the Muslim ruler, where he was granted an audience. He outlined the philosophy and importance of nonharming. Then he advocated on behalf of the animals. "Cows give us milk, so they are like our mother. Bulls help to plow fields to produce food grains, so they are like our father. Killing these cows and bulls to eat meat is like killing our mother and father and eating their meat." The ruler was moved by Chaitanya's philosophy and lifestyle. He ordered an end to the killing of cows and bulls, becoming an ardent practitioner of nonharming and nonviolence.

Without being overly dogmatic about the killing and eating of animals, those who want to pursue a deeper spiritual path must wrestle with this issue. At its core, vegetarianism is a lifestyle that embodies nonviolence, nonkilling, and nonharming. As you consider your own path to a more authentic spiritual life, reflect on ways that you can embrace the principle of nonharming. A commitment to ethical and spiritual living will always involve some kind of effort to fulfill the precept of reverence for all life.

NONHARMING (Part 2)

EXTENDING COMPASSION TO ALL CREATURES.

> *No civilization is complete which does not include*
> *the dumb and defenseless of God's creatures within the*
> *sphere of charity and mercy.*
> —QUEEN VICTORIA

Ask yourself this personal question: *How would I treat animals if I viewed them as people?*

The wisdom that comes from the East consistently reminds humans to extend their compassion, kindness, and generosity to all sentient beings, which includes animals, birds, fish, insects, etc. Here is a story that powerfully reinforces that lesson, and reminds us that the divine resides within all creatures, not only human beings.

Many generations ago, there was a devout man whose daily prayer was this: "God, I want you to come in person to visit me and have a meal with me, my family, my friends." Because of his persistence, God appeared to him, saying, "Very well, I'll come and join you for a meal." Overjoyed, the man responded, "Wonderful, wonderful. When will you come? I need to know so that I can prepare everything."

"I'll come on Friday, at noon," God said before disappearing.

The man invited everyone he knew and began preparing a sumptuous meal. On Friday at noon, a huge dining table was set up. Everyone he invited was present and patiently waiting outside the dining room. However, when the clock struck noon and God was not present, the man was puzzled. "I know God didn't lie to me. He said he would be here at noon."

Somewhat confused but still hopeful, the man decided to wait another half hour as a courtesy. Still, God did not show. His guests began complaining, "You fool, you told us God would be here for lunch. We had doubts and now we know. Why would God come and eat with you? Come on, let's leave."

The man pleaded, "No, wait." He went into the dining room to think. To his consternation he saw a large black dog on the dining table, eating everything in sight. "Oh no," he lamented. "God saw the dog eating his food and chose not to come." So, the man grabbed a club and began beating the dog mercilessly. In pain, the creature limped away. Then the man came out to his guests, explaining, "It's not my fault. Neither God nor you can eat, because the food was polluted by the dog. That's why God didn't come." His guests left, and the man retreated to pray over his disappointment. During his prayer God appeared to him once again, but this time there were wounds and bruises all over his body. As God walked, he limped.

"What happened to you?" the man asked. "You must have gotten into a terrible accident."

"It was no accident," God said. "You did this to me."

Mortified, the man said, "Why are you blaming me? I didn't do that to you."

"Yes you did," God insisted. "I arrived for the meal promptly at noon and began eating. Then you came in and beat me with a club. You struck and struck, causing these wounds and bruises."

"But you weren't there," the man protested.

"Are you sure no one was eating the food?" God asked.

"Well, yes, there was a large black dog."

"That was me," God said. "I really wanted to enjoy the meal, so I came as a hungry dog."

Once again, ask yourself this personal question: *How would I treat animals if I viewed them as people?*

OPENNESS

CULTIVATING AN OPEN MIND.

Those who are open-eyed are open-minded;
those who are open-minded are open-hearted.
—LAO TZU

An older woman was sitting by the road outside her village when she was approached by a traveler, who asked, "What kind of people live in this village?"

"What were the people like in your home village?" she asked in turn.

"Oh, they were terrible!" complained the traveler. "The entire village was filled with liars, cheats, incompetents. Not one of them could be trusted. It was impossible to make friends. I was glad to leave."

"You'll find the people in this village are just the same," said the older woman.

A short time later she was approached by a second traveler, who raised the same question: "What kind of people make up this village?"

"What were the people like in your home village?" she asked again.

"Oh, they were wonderful," exclaimed the traveler. "Kind, good, honest, hard-working. It was a privilege to live there. I was so sorry to leave."

"You'll find the people in this town are just the same," she said.

This story is told in the East to demonstrate the power of perception and personality to shape expectation. The two travelers represent the two kinds of personalities present in each one of us. When we are filled with negativity, distrust, and fear, we view the world and those in it as unfriendly, inhospitable, combative, malicious, cold-hearted. We are world-denying. On the other hand, when we are filled with love, kindness, compassion, understanding, and a great faith in humanity, we view the world and those in it as friendly, inviting, beautiful, inspiring, and helpful. In this mode we are world-affirming. Our stance is open, with our arms wide enough to embrace all whom we encounter.

The saying from Lao Tzu is quite correct: "Those who are open-eyed are open-minded; those who are open-minded are open-hearted." The flip side of his observation is equally correct: "Those who are closed-eyed are closed-minded; those who are closed-minded are closed-hearted." At any given moment we can be open or closed. The key to living a healthy and robust spiritual life is to tip the balance in favor of being more and more consistently open. As we do that, we are much more likely to see the Buddha or the Christ in every person we meet, and far less likely to see others as competitors and enemies.

POSSESSIONS

ARE YOU POSSESSED BY YOUR POSSESSIONS?

I slept and dreamt that life was joy.
I awoke and saw that life was service.
I acted and behold, service was joy.

—RABINDRANATH TAGORE

While traveling through India, a woman had a dream in which she was instructed to ask a beggar for a gift. Because the dream was so vivid and urgent, the woman acted on it. The next morning she approached the first beggar she encountered, an old man, asking him for a gift. Without hesitation, the old man reached into his sack and pulled out a huge diamond. It was larger than a tomato.

"This is all I have," he said, "so this must be the gift mentioned in your dream. Please take it."

Astonished, the woman responded, "Do you know what you're doing in giving this away?"

"Yes, of course," the man replied. "I found this in the swamp just outside the city."

The woman thanked the beggar for his gift and went to the swamp, where she spent the entire day in meditation. As the sun began to fall, she returned to the beggar, thanked him for his gift, and then returned the diamond to him, saying, "Instead of this diamond, could you please teach me the wisdom that freed you to give me this gift?"

This story reveals the two types of people in the world. One group is possessed by their possessions. They are driven, always seeking and grasping after more and more. The other, a much smaller group, is possessed by the spirit of service, of compassion, of sharing. This spirit drives them to serve others with abandon. What they possess, they freely share. Into which group would you be placed?

PRACTICE

PRACTICING THE EIGHTFOLD PATH IN DAILY LIFE.

> *No horse gets anywhere until he is harnessed. No steam or*
> *gas ever drives anything until it is confined. No Niagara is*
> *ever turned into light and power until it is tunneled. No*
> *life ever grows great until it is focused, dedicated, disciplined.*
> —HARRY EMERSON FOSDICK

Every faith tradition stresses the importance of disciplined spiritual practices. Central to the practice of Buddhism is the discipline of following the Eightfold Path taught by the Buddha himself:

1. *Right understanding*
2. *Right purpose*
3. *Right speech*
4. *Right action*
5. *Right livelihood*
6. *Right effort*

7. *Right mindfulness*

8. *Right concentration*

This ancient Buddhist teaching applies amazingly well and naturally to many of the dilemmas we deal with in our daily lives. Suppose you are having trouble with relationships and feel that you have no success in them. The Buddhist Eightfold Path can provide wisdom for shaping and structuring even our romantic relationships. Before making a major commitment to a partner and investing massive amounts of emotional energy, it can help to step back and use the Eightfold Path to assess whether or not the person you're drawn to will make a good lifelong partner.

1. *Right understanding:* Does he have basic common sense and sensitivity?

2. *Right purpose:* Does she have worthy personal and professional goals?

3. *Right speech:* Does he say what he means and mean what he says?

4. *Right action:* Is she an ethical person; is she honest and trustworthy?

5. *Right livelihood:* Does he have a good and healthy work ethic?

6. *Right effort:* Does she try to do her best?

7. *Right mindfulness:* Is he capable of self-reflection and inner growth?

8. *Right concentration:* Is she a good listener? When you're upset, can she focus on what you're saying and feeling? Is she truly empathetic?

If you answered "no" to many of these questions, then you'd be wise to be cautious about pursuing the relationship.

Another way to apply the Eightfold Path is toward yourself—this is something one ought to do frequently. You can use it to do a self-study to determine whether or not you are growing both emotionally and spiritually. Catholic readers might recognize this approach as an "examination of conscience," a tool often recommended by

Catholic spiritual leaders. Here's how it works when using Buddha's Eightfold Path:

1. *Right understanding:* Do I truly try to understand others, what they feel, and where they are coming from? Do I honestly attempt to walk in their shoes?

2. *Right purpose:* Is my life fulfilling? Am I doing what I really want, or am I doing simply what has come along? Am I living a purposeful life?

3. *Right speech:* Do I use words to hurt or heal, to burden or bless others? When I make a promise, do I keep it?

4. *Right action:* Do I try to be skillful when responding to those around me—family, friends, colleagues—seeking to make things better rather than worse?

5. *Right livelihood:* Am I engaged in work and activities that bring me satisfaction and that are meaningful for the community?

6. *Right effort:* Are the people in my life good for me or bad for me? Do they lift me up or pull me down? When I've accepted a responsibility—whether it's professional or personal—am I trying to do my best?

7. *Right mindfulness:* Do I try always to see the best, hope for the best, and work for the best in all things?

8. *Right concentration:* Do I read materials that facilitate my inner growth, or am I reading merely to be entertained and fill time? When I am in the presence of others who can teach me things, do I pay attention? Do I listen carefully and try to learn from them?

These are just a few ways the Eightfold Path can be put into daily practice. It's an enormously useful tool for helping us to know ourselves better and to understand and deal with life's complexities in a clearer way.

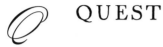

QUEST

THE REAL QUEST IN LIFE.

> *If, moment by moment, you can keep your mind clear,*
> *then nothing can stop you.*
> —SHENG YEN

After winning one archery contest after another, a young champion was experiencing a confidence which bordered on arrogance. Boasting about his skill as an archer, he challenged a Zen master who was also well known for his archery. The younger man demonstrated his truly remarkable proficiency when he hit a distant bull's eye and then split that arrow with his second shot. "There," he said to the older Zen master, "see if you can match that!"

Undisturbed and without speaking, the master did not draw his bow but motioned for the young man to follow him. Together they made their way up a mountain. Curious about the older man's intention, the younger archer followed him high into the mountain. Finally they reached an area where a deep chasm was spanned by a rather flimsy, old, rotting and shaky log. Calmly stepping out into the middle of the unsteady and potentially perilous bridge, the old master picked a far-away tree as a target. He drew his bow, firing a direct clean hit. Gracefully stepping off the log he said: "Now it's your turn." Staring in fear at the seemingly bottomless and beckoning abyss, the young man could not force himself to step out onto the log, no less shoot at any target.

After a few moments, the Zen master said: "You have much skill with your bow and arrow but you have little skill with the mind that lets loose the shot."

That episode was the Zen master's way of reminding the young archer that the real quest in life is to train the mind; to function in all areas of life with a skillful mind. Such a quest is a lifelong goal and one which is supreme over all other achievements. The mind can work with us or against us. The mind is our most powerful weapon. That's why modern Buddhist teacher Sheng Yen (born in 1945) taught: *If, moment by moment, you can keep your mind clear, then nothing can stop you.* Clarity of mind and skillful thinking is the real quest in life.

REINCARNATION

You are born again and again and again . . .

> *Reincarnation is a series of dreams within a dream:*
> *man's individual dreams within the greater dream of God.*
> —Paramahansa Yogananda

Simply defined, reincarnation is the re-birth of a soul in another body. For some, the concept of reincarnation is merely a myth, or at worst, a ludicrous concept. Yet, throughout history and all over the East, reincarnation was and continues to be regarded as being completely in line with the natural laws of the universe, whereby nothing is lost or wasted and everything is recycled. Here are some brief thoughts on reincarnation:

• Death is not a final point, but an exit point when the soul is reborn (or recycled) in another body.

• Reincarnation follows universal laws of natural cycles.

• Reincarnation is a gracious act of God or the Divine, giving us several opportunities to make corrections in our thinking and behavior.

• Through reincarnation we are given time to relive past experiences in order to make good that which was bad and to make better that which was good.

• The goal in returning and being reborn is improvement to the point of perfection. When that takes place we become one with the Divine.

• The concept of reincarnation appears several times in the Bible. Some examples include: Matthew 17:10-13, where Jesus implies that John the Baptist was the reincarnation of the Jewish prophet Elijah; Matthew 16:14, where Jesus is believed to be the reincarnation of John the Baptist or the prophet Jeremiah or the prophet Elijah. Also, the apostle Paul appears to teach a form of reincarnation: "God cannot be mocked. A man reaps what he sows" (Gal. 6:7). Many see this text as a classic expression of karma. Another reflection of the karmic law of action and consequences appears in this word of Jesus: "All who draw the sword will die by the sword" (Matt. 26:52).

• Some of the biggest names in early Christianity believed in and taught reincarnation. These include Origen (185-254), Justin Martyr (100-165), Irenaeus (130-200), Tertullian (145-220), and Gregory of Nyssa (335-395). It was the fifth ecumenical council of 533 which eventually condemned the teaching of reincarnation, in spite of the fact that it had been strongly advocated by earlier Christian leaders.

To repeat, the point of reincarnation, of being born again and again, is correction and improvement. One of the finest expressions of this concept can be seen in a parable *There's A Hole In My Sidewalk,* written by Portia Nelson, which reads:

Chapter One
I walk down a street and there's a big hole. I don't see it
and fall into it. It's dark and hopeless and it takes me a long
time to find my way out. It's not my fault!

Chapter Two
I walk down the same street. There's a big hole and I can see it, but I still fall in. It's dark and hopeless and it takes me a long time to get out. It's still not my fault.

Chapter Three
I walk down a street. There's a big hole. I can see it, but I still fall in. It's become a habit. But I keep my eyes open and get out immediately. It is my fault.

Chapter Four
I walk down a street. There's a big hole. I walk around it.

Chapter Five
I walk down a different street.

RELIGION

BEING RELIGIOUSLY TOLERANT.

> *[Eastern] philosophy consists of three propositions.*
> *First, that Man's real nature is divine. Second, that the aim*
> *of human life is to realize this divine nature. Third, that all*
> *religions are essentially in agreement.*
>
> —CHRISTOPHER ISHERWOOD

Religious tolerance is sadly absent on our planet, and religious conflict has thus become the source of much upheaval and tragedy. Consider how much of the world's suffering and pain would be alleviated if people could act on the truth of Christopher Isherwood's statement "all religions are essentially in agreement." One who experienced this truth and then taught it to his own disciples was the great Bengali spiritual leader Ramakrishna Paramahansa (1836-1886). Today he is worshipped by many Hindus as an avatar, a divine incarnation. For those Hindus he is what Jesus, the God-man, is to Christians.

Born to very poor parents, Ramakrishna received little schooling, but because of his deep interest in spiritual growth he became a priest at a Kali temple in 1856. There he studied for twelve years under the guidance of various gurus. It quickly became evident that Ramakrishna was deeply devoted and highly talented in the discipline of spirituality. He was able to enter higher states of consciousness which took other yogis a lifetime to master. His favorite deity was the goddess Kali, to whom he had an enthusiastic devotion. Because of his spirituality, Ramakrishna attracted many disciples. One of his most famous disciples was Swami Vivekananda, who would travel to the United States in 1893, where he addressed the World Parliament of Religions, making such a positive impression that Hindu religion and philosophy began to penetrate American minds.

As Ramakrishna's fame spread, he created a sudden crisis of faith for his followers when he converted to Islam. Always curious about expressions of faith wherever he saw them, Ramakrishna engaged in a conversation with a Sufi who had come to view the temple. As the two spoke, Ramakrishna was so impressed by the man's piety and teachings of Islam that he declared, "Islam is also a way to reach God. I will practice this path." To the absolute shock of his family, friends, and disciples, he quit coming to the temple. Ramakrishna dressed like a Muslim, performed the Islamic prayers five times a day while bowing toward Mecca, and refused to acknowledge any of the Hindu gods. He further stunned his followers by announcing he would change his diet and eat like a Muslim. That meant eating beef, an appalling act for a culture that regards the cow as a sacred creature never to be harmed. This was too much for his disciples, who quickly employed a Muslim cook, instructing him to prepare a completely vegetarian meal served Muslim-style. Because Ramakrishna had never tasted beef, he ate the meal none the wiser.

After three days of total surrender to Islam, Ramakrishna experienced a vision in which he saw the prophet Mohammed. He was shining as an intensely bright light, which dissolved into God, and then God dissolved into Absolute Reality.

Ramakrishna again entered into one of his states of higher consciousness, and his disciples had difficulty bringing him back into an earthly presence. When he came out of this state, Ramakrishna taught his followers: "Islam is a true path. I experienced the highest reality by practicing it." With that statement he began again to practice his Hindu faith. Of course, his family, friends, and disciples were immensely relieved.

Their relief, however, was short-lived, for soon a Christian visited the temple, telling Ramakrishna about Jesus, or *Isha* as he is known among Hindus. It would be hard to imagine what Ramakrishna's followers thought when he announced that he would now follow the Christian path. True to his word, he began intense meditation before an icon of the Virgin Mary, holding the baby *Isha* in her lap. As he meditated, Ramakrishna again entered into a state of higher consciousness.

Not long after he embraced Christianity, Ramakrishna had another vision in which he saw a foreigner with a radiant face. The man in his vision walked directly toward Ramakrishna. "This is Jesus Christ!" he realized. The radiant figure continued walking toward Ramakrishna and then merged into his heart. Once more Ramakrishna entered an ecstatic state. His followers' anxieties were greatly reduced when Ramakrishna returned to Hinduism, resuming his duties as a priest of Kali. However, he now taught people: "Christianity is a true faith too. If you practice Christianity sincerely, it will take you to God."

In this one man we see a person who tested and practiced three of the world's great religions and found them to be legitimate spiritual paths. In spite of differences of culture, practice, and theological expression, each faith leads to the ultimate reality we call God. The lessons we need to learn from Ramakrishna are to practice religious tolerance and to sincerely follow your chosen deity.

REQUIRING MORE

Pulling out the arrows.

You must push yourself beyond your limits,
all the time.

An Eastern story tells about a man who had been struck by a poisoned arrow. That same day, he encountered the Buddha and began to complain bitterly about his condition. The Buddha listened and then said, "You can spend your time lamenting who shot you or you could pull out the arrow! Right now, what would be the better course of action?"

If the wounded man was listening, he would have learned this important life lesson from the Buddha: we must require more of ourselves. In his case, he chose to become fixated on his problem. He was committed to feeling victimized and to lamenting the unfairness of life. Because he narrowed his vision, it never occurred to him that he could take action. He could remove the arrow and begin to heal.

There are many times when we, like that man, are wounded, either by the deliberate action of another person or simply as a casualty of random events. When those moments occur rather than complain, lament, accuse, protest, gripe, and find fault, we must require more from ourselves. By demanding more from ourselves, we stretch, expand our emotional boundaries, and, ultimately, heal from the wound. Here are ways of requiring more from yourself:

- Require more resilience from yourself. Tell yourself you can and will overcome.
- Require more insight from yourself. Tell yourself that you will find the opportunity present in the adversity.
- Require more trust from yourself. Tell yourself that you have friends and family who want to help you heal. Trust them and let them give you the support you need to get through the difficulty.
- Require more persistence from yourself. Tell yourself you will survive and rebuild your life in spite of loss and pain.
- Require more action from yourself. Today, begin to develop plans and strategies for effectively dealing with issues that you face.

REVERENCE

EXPANDING REVERENCE FOR LIFE

The good man is a friend of all living things.
—MAHATMA GANDHI

One Saturday morning I arrived at the gym for a workout. As I walked by the reception desk, the clerk welcomed me warmly, then suddenly leapt up and began running down the hallway. I was alarmed, believing some crisis needed his immediate attention. However, the reason for his dash turned out to be a small black cricket that had entered the building. To my utter dismay, the gym worker ran, stopped, and promptly stepped on the cricket, ending its life instantly.

On the surface, his action could be interpreted as harmless. Yet, if we probe deeper, some troubling questions can be raised: *Was it necessary to kill the cricket? Why was his immediate response to run and destroy a small, harmless insect? What is it in our culture and our upbringing that permits us to act harmfully without any pang of conscience or remorse? Why did he not simply scoop up the little creature in a tissue and carry it outside, where it could live and flourish?*

The action taken by that gym employee is not uncommon in the West. We grow up squashing bugs and insects without giving it a second thought. In the East, however, a vastly different perspective is encouraged, one that should pose a challenge to the typical Western view. Consider the encounter two little American boys had with an elderly Buddhist monk, who was visiting the United States from Thailand. Because of the monk's reputation as a meditation teacher, he was asked to offer a series of classes. At one such event, a young mother was present with her two boys, aged eight and eleven. Following the lecture, the monk and the woman were conversing as the children watched with some boredom. A mosquito landed on the monk's arm and began to probe for blood. Someone was about to whisk it away when the monk shook his head, saying quietly, "It takes so little."

The young boys, who had been disinterested in the event, suddenly focused intensely on the monk. Evidently, the thought of *not* killing a biting mosquito had never occurred to them. The monk, noting their interest, used the moment to instruct them in the philosophy of reverence for *all* life. Addressing them directly, he said, "All living things wish to live and be happy."

Eastern religions and philosophies all strongly emphasize reverence for *all* life—human, animal, insect—all living creatures come under the reverence for life umbrella. This philosophy is clearly articulated in the *Kan-Ying-P'ien,* known in English as *The Book of Actions and Rewards.* Dating back to the Sung Dynasty (960-1280 CE), it contains 212 short ethical maxims, which include: "Have a pitiful heart for all creatures" and "One must bring no sorrow even on worms, plants and trees." Behind those injunctions is the deep conviction that all things wish to live. Even deeper, however, is the concern that when we act callously toward even these smallest of life forms, that callousness can grow into larger cruelties. Thus *The Book of*

Actions and Rewards also exhorts: "Do not allow your children to amuse themselves by playing with flies or butterflies or little birds. It is not merely that such proceeding may result in damage to living creatures; they waken in young hearts the inclination to cruelty and murder."

Of course, it's a huge leap from squashing a cricket to taking a human life. Just think, though, how much kinder and gentler our culture could be if reverence for *all* of life were emphasized in the home, at school, from pulpits and lecterns. Gandhi is absolutely correct when he observed that the good person is a friend of all living things. Today, be a good person and help others under your sphere of influence to be equally good.

SCRIPTURE

THE IMPORTANCE OF SCRIPTURE STUDY.

Outside the room gain knowledge;
inside the room gain wisdom.

—CHUANG TZU

One of the most important and influential Jewish teachers was the second-century Rabbi Akiva. Unlike many other spiritual leaders, Rabbi Akiva did not come from a lineage of teachers. In fact, he remained illiterate until well into middle age. One rabbinic tale recounts how Akiva became the inspired and inspiring *Rabbi Akiva*: "He was forty years old and had not yet learned a thing. Once he stood at the mouth of a well and asked, 'Who hollowed this stone?' He was told, 'Is it not the water which constantly falls on it day after day?' Rabbi Akiva immediately reasoned, 'If soft water can wear away hard stone, how much more can the words of the Torah, which are as hard as iron, carve a way into my heart, which is of flesh and blood?'"

Later, Abba Poemen, a Christian Desert Father, made a similar discovery about the impact of scripture study. "The nature of water is yielding and that of a stone is hard," he explained. "Yet if you hang a bottle filled with water above the stone so that the water drips drop by drop, it will wear a hole in the stone. In the same way the word of God is tender, and our heart is hard. So when people hear the word of God frequently, their hearts are opened to the reverence of God."

Both Rabbi Akiva and Abba Poemen stressed the importance of studying sacred texts. All of the world's religions have developed scriptures or wisdom literature that can guide us in our spiritual growth. There are the Bhagavad Gita and the Upanishads in Hinduism, the Tao Te Ching in Taoism, the Analects of Confucianism, the Hebrew and Christian Bibles, the Muslim Koran, the Dhammapada of Buddhism, and many, many more.

It is the study of sacred texts that will allow us to go deeper in our spirituality, to move from the "outside room" to the "inside room," to gain wisdom, rather than just knowledge and information. But for any scripture to leave its mark on our spirit, to transform us, that scripture must be studied consistently. Commenting on Rabbi Akiva's experience, the nineteenth-century Rabbi Israel Salanter said: "The waters carved the stone only because it fell, drop after drop, year after year, without pause. Had the accumulated water all poured down at once in a powerful stream, it would have slipped off the rock without leaving a trace."

It is not enough to hear a sacred text read in a religious service from time to time. What is most beneficial for spiritual growth is permitting a scripture to carve its way into our hearts, minds, and spirits. For that to happen, we must study the text in a disciplined fashion, day after day, just as Rabbi Akiva did. So, find a text you like—it could be the Psalms of the Hebrew Bible, the Gospels of the Christian Bible, the Analects of Confucius, the sayings of the Buddha. And, if you adhere closely to one faith, consider doing a study of a sacred text from a faith different from yours. Find a text you are drawn to, and then make it your daily practice to read it, study it, and meditate on it. Little by little, your spiritual life will expand, and your life will be transformed.

SEEING

SEEING THE POTENTIAL, NOT THE PROBLEM.

If your daily life seems poor, do not blame it;
blame yourself, tell yourself that you are not poet
enough to call forth its riches.

—RAINER MARIA RILKE

There is a legend about a great king who ruled a small country. His kingdom was not a superpower, nor would it ever be one. The country had limited resources, much poverty, and low levels of education. There was, however, one enormous source of national pride. The king had a large, perfect diamond that had been passed down through his family for many generations. Wanting to share it with his citizens, the king kept it on display so that all who wished could come to see and appreciate the beauty of this flawless gem. People came from around the kingdom to admire it.

One day, the head of security, who was responsible for protecting the diamond, came to the king with the unhappy news that the diamond had developed a large crack. The head of security explained that no one had touched the diamond, as it was carefully guarded night and day. The king rushed to see it himself, and sure enough, there was a crack right through the middle of the stone.

Of course, the king immediately summoned the kingdom's finest jewelers, asking them to examine the diamond. They studied the gem and, without exception, all told the king the same bad news: "The diamond is useless and worthless. It is irredeemably flawed."

The king was crushed, as was the nation. With their source of pride gone, the nation's self-esteem plummeted. "We are just a small, poor country, insignificant among the world's nations," they lamented.

Then, along came an old man who was not known by anyone in the king's court, nor by any of the jewelers. The man claimed that he too was a jeweler, and asked if he could examine the diamond. After carefully scrutinizing the gem, he confidently told the king, "I can fix it. In fact, I can make it better than it was before." The king was shocked. He was leery of this stranger and unsure how to respond. "Give me the diamond, and in a week I'll bring it back better than it was before," the man requested.

Unwilling to let the stone out of his sight, even if it was ruined, the king countered, telling the man he would provide him with a workroom in the palace along with all the tools he needed, as well as food and drink. Then the king waited, as did the entire kingdom. It was a very long week for them. After seven days, the man appeared with the stone in his hand. He gave it to the king, who was overwhelmed by what he saw. It was breathtaking and magnificent. The king couldn't believe his eyes. Using the crack that ran through the middle of the stone as a stem, the old jeweler carved an intricate, full-blown rose, complete with leaves and thorns, into the diamond. It was an exquisite work of art.

So overjoyed was the king that he offered the old man a great reward saying, "You have taken something beautiful and perfect and improved upon it." The old man refused all gifts and honors, saying to the king and his advisors: "I didn't do that at all. What I did was to take something flawed and cracked at its heart and turn it into something beautiful."

So many of us have eyes, but don't see. So many of us easily see the flaw, the imperfection, the cracks in life but never see the possibilities present. Perhaps today is a good day to begin training our eyes and our spirits to see the potential that presents itself in every problem we encounter in ourselves and in others.

SELF

Taming the self.

Get rid of the self and act from the Self.
—Zen saying

An ancient emperor was the ruler of a large and vast land. He was greatly troubled, because things seemed to go from bad to worse under his rule. Revolt, wars, and famine ravaged his people. Even within his own court of advisors, there was tension, disagreement, conflict, intrigue. He was aware that some were plotting to overthrow him. His advisors were of no help, because they had all become "yes" people, merely saying what they thought he wanted to hear. Each of the advisors continually assured the emperor, saying "You were born under a lucky star and will rule well" and "The stars all point to great success and longevity for you and your rule."

The emperor, however, was not fooled. He knew something was drastically wrong. Unable to receive honest counsel, he decided to visit a famous mystic and monk who lived in the mountains. The monk was highly regarded—almost revered—by the common people. Because it was a journey that would take many days, winding through paths frequented by bandits, he made the trip with an armed escort. Finally, the group reached the cave where they were told the sage resided. Ordering his guard to remain behind, the emperor said he would go alone into the cave.

Inside, the emperor found the cave empty. He was deeply disappointed. But on the way down from the cave, he encountered an old man seated and meditating by the path. Thinking he had found the sage, the emperor knelt before him, asking advice on how to better rule his empire. The old man seemed not to hear the emperor, and continued to sit quietly in meditation. The emperor concluded that the man was not the sage he was looking for, and began to leave, feeling badly that his quest for the sage had ended unsuccessfully.

As he turned away to leave, the emperor noticed something extraordinary. Initially, he had thought that the man was sitting on a rock beside the path. However, the man was actually floating, levitating, a few inches above the ground. The emperor knew, without a doubt, that he had found the man he was looking for, and pleaded with him for his insight on how to rule the vast empire. "I only know how to rule my own life," the sage finally said. "I don't know anything about ruling a country." Then he closed his eyes and fell back into his meditative state.

Pressing the sage further, the emperor said, "I need your help. My empire is about to fall into ruins and my people depend upon me to provide security and stability. Yet, I often feel confused and conflicted about the way to do this for the common good of all. I have spoken to many counselors and advisors but cannot find the way to be the ruler that I wish to be."

The sage suddenly opened his eyes, paused briefly and then spoke: "Only someone who can manage his own life—his own self—can manage an entire land." Pausing a second time, the sage added, "I see before me a man who is deeply conflicted, filled with doubt, and overly dependent on the opinion and advice of others. If your life is in turmoil, how can you expect to properly rule over the nation?"

Immediately, the emperor felt as though an enormous burden had been removed from him. He understood the sage's insight, realizing that if he were to rule successfully, he would first have to know himself and tame the self. Thus, he left the old monk and began a lifelong journey of self-reflection, through lengthy periods of meditation that heightened his self-awareness and allowed him to tap into his own depths. He became more centered and more focused; he experienced more clarity about complex issues and became far less reliant on the opinions of others. Gradually, his empire was unified and the people enjoyed a time of great peace and prosperity.

That ancient tale is a reminder that we need to "get rid of the self and act from the Self"; that is, we need to act from our deeper, more authentic self. If we are constantly agitated, angry, and tense, we are more likely to bring those qualities out in the people around us, even those whom we love and value. Those negative emotions are merely on the surface of the "self." If we challenge ourselves to dig deeper into our psyche, into our true "Self," we will encounter there a vast wisdom and a vast place of peace and love. That wisdom, peace, and love can be brought to the surface, displacing agitation, anger, and tension.

SPIRITUALITY

ASSESSING YOUR SPIRITUAL IQ.

> *Once we have the condition of peace and joy in us, we can*
> *afford to be in any situation. Even in the situation of hell,*
> *we will be able to contribute our peace and serenity.*
> —THICH NHAT HANH

Unfortunately, Western culture is not particularly supportive of spiritual life and practices. Should a young man or woman in their late teens announce that they wanted to go off alone to meditate and pursue a spiritual life, their family and friends would be concerned, even alarmed. Yet in the East, such a young person would be encouraged and even revered for their pursuit of a deeper spiritual life. In spite of the fact that Western culture lacks the supportive outlook of the East when it comes to spiritual development, many people are commendably working at cultivating their inner lives.

All of which raises the question: *How does a person assess his or her spiritual IQ?* Here are some Eastern strategies for assessing your progress in spiritual awareness and growth. The degree to which your spirit informs your living is rising when you:

• are looking and asking for guidance concerning spiritual growth; your methods include finding a supportive spiritual environment, reading inspiring books, and learning from gifted spiritual teachers;

• increasingly experience the "condition of peace and joy" spoken of by Thich Nhat Hanh, and bring it to others who are troubled, distressed, or hurting;

• are living and acting more from interior convictions than to gain the approval of others;

• forgive more easily those who have hurt you—an ex-spouse, a parent, a teacher, a coach;

• cultivate self-discipline in matters large and small;

• wake up on many days feeling grateful—even very, very grateful for no reason other than the opportunity to enjoy another day;

• are more able to speak the truth in love and gentleness;

• notice that you are not as upset by life's dilemmas and difficulties; you remain calm in the midst of chaos;

• realize that you don't need to control outcomes, that you can speak and act on your best impulses without being caught up in the end result;

• have the ability to look for deeper meaning in events;

• are becoming more and more compassionate, kind, accepting, and loving;

• commit to engaging in regular spiritual practices such as meditation, prayer, and study;

• understand that spirituality is not something you do, but who you are and how you live;

• exhibit humility in your spiritual growth, avoiding pretense and self-inflation;

• are no longer possessed by your possessions;

• experience concern and compassion not only for other people but for animals, plants, and the earth itself;

• seek to help others to develop spiritually;

• feel a growing understanding and appreciation of your essence, your Buddha-nature, the Christ within you, or the divine presence, which is your true inner self.

SUFFERING

Changing our relationship to pain.

Rather than give the body relief, give relief to the mind:
when the mind is at peace, the body is not distressed.
—Yamada Mumon

The following is a very well-known story, but is cited here because its deeper meaning is often missed. Kisa Gotami's daughter died, leaving her mother in agony over the loss. Kisa's grief felt unbearable and manifested itself in body and mind. Desperately seeking relief, she remembered that the Buddha was capable of miracles. So she approached the Buddha, pleading for her daughter to be brought back to life. The Buddha, filled with compassion for Kisa, promised he would help her, but on one condition: she needed to bring him some mustard seed from a home that had never experienced sorrow.

Filled with new hope, Kisa set off on a search. "This should not be difficult," she thought. She knew that mustard seed was a common spice found in almost every home in the village. However, as she knocked on door after door, she heard one sad story after another. Every time she asked, "Has there been suffering and sorrow in this home?" she heard a new tale of pain:

"Oh, yes, Grandfather died last year."

"Yes, my son was born with a clubfoot and is unable to walk."

"My mother is desperately ill and will soon die."

"I lost two daughters in childbirth and have just miscarried again."

"My husband, the father of our four children, was killed in an accident."

It was not long before Kisa realized that suffering was universal. No human being could escape loss and sorrow. Kisa reflected on her experience and on the Buddha's suggestion to find mustard seed from a home that had never experienced sorrow. Before long, she returned to the Buddha, becoming one of his earliest and most devoted followers.

The usual interpretation of this story is to say that Kisa's grief was eased simply because she discovered that others suffer as well. However, there is more to glean from that famous story. Simply knowing that other people experience loss was not enough to remove Kisa's grief. The loss of a child is, after all, one of life's harshest blows, and one from which some people never rebound. Obviously something happened to Kisa as a result of her search, and it was this: *Her new perspective—that suffering is universal—changed her relationship to her pain.* The pain was still there, but it was no longer the driving force of her thoughts and actions. She had been clinging tightly to the view that her child should not have died, that life dealt her an unfair blow, that she should have had the opportunity to see her daughter grow up, marry, have children, and so on. She victimized herself by wishing her world would be as it once was.

Somehow, the realization that suffering is found in all lives altered her perspective, changing her relationship with her pain. Although Kisa probably missed her daughter all of her life, the anguish and anger of the loss receded. By understanding deeply that suffering is universal, she was able to free herself from her pain and begin to experience hope and joy along with her loss and grief.

The lesson that the Buddha hoped Kisa would learn is one we need to absorb today whenever events come our way that we label "unfortunate" and "tragic." We will still suffer, but if we can hold off attaching more emotional turmoil to the issue, then we can be free of the pain our attachments create. This insight is also demonstrated in a more current setting in the following story.

A school system in a large city had a special program to help hospitalized children keep up with their schoolwork. One day, a teacher who worked in the program received a routine call asking her to visit such a child. She was given the child's name, hospital, and room number. Her instructions were to help the boy with lessons in grammar.

That same day, the teacher went to see the boy. No one had mentioned to her that the youth had been badly burned and was in great pain. Caught off guard by the boy's disfiguring burns, his bandaged face, and his obvious physical pain, she struggled through the lesson. When she left the hospital room, the teacher was disappointed with herself, feeling that she had not accomplished much with her hospitalized student.

However, upon returning the next day, a nurse asked her: "What did you do with that boy? Ever since you visited yesterday, his attitude toward recovery has improved." The teacher was quite surprised, and listened carefully as the nurse explained that the entire staff was worried about the youth. He had not been responding effectively to treatment, nor was he showing much improvement. "After your visit, he became more responsive to treatment. It's as though he's decided to live," the nurse explained. The explanation for the boy's remarkable transformation came two weeks later, when the boy quietly explained that he had completely given up hope until the teacher arrived. Everything changed when he came to a simple realization, which he expressed this way: "They wouldn't send a teacher to work with me on grammar if I was dying, would they?"

Elements of that story are worth examining closely. At the end of the story, the boy is still in physical pain. The sight of his burns is no less disturbing and frightening. Bandages over his face continue to keep him in the dark. Yet, even in the darkness, he begins to experience the light of hope. This story makes this crucial point: *It is the boy's relationship to his pain that has changed, and that has relieved him of feeling hopeless.* Especially insightful is the nurse's statement about the boy: "It's as though he's decided to live." Her comment brings out the truth that the attitude we take toward our painful situations is a matter of choice. We can either lay more emotional baggage onto our traumas, or we can accept what has happened. Without the additional emotional baggage, we are free to deal with the matter in a rational, healthy, constructive, and balanced way.

TEACHERS

RECOGNIZING TEACHERS.

> *When walking in the company of two other men, I am bound to be able to learn from them. The good points of one I copy; the bad points of the other I correct in myself.*
> —CONFUCIUS

The name "Confucius" is an English transliteration of K'ung Fu Tzu (551-479 BCE), the great Chinese sage. It is impossible to understand Chinese history and culture without a deep encounter with Confucius and his teaching, which shaped Chinese social, cultural, and political history for twenty-four hundred years, until the Communist revolution of the 1940s. Although Confucius was more of an ethical and moral teacher than a spiritual leader, his philosophy reflects many spiritual teachings from Buddhism and Taoism. He is one of the most important teachers in the history of civilization: his influence in the East is comparable to the influence of Plato and Aristotle in the West. His philosophy has a huge impact not only on China, but on Japan, Korea and Vietnam as well.

Not given to abstract philosophical musings, Confucius emphasized the practical over the theoretical. He dealt with concrete problems that are often absent in traditional Eastern religions such as Buddhism and Hinduism. Among his concerns are those that most of us encounter daily: What is the proper role of government? What are the best ways for families to get along? What is necessary for a society to run smoothly and fairly? One of Confucius' important lessons, applicable for us today, is that of recognizing teachers. If Confucius were alive today, he would remind us that we can and ought to see everyone as our teacher. If we choose to, we can observe all those who enter our lives and learn from them. Those who have admirable qualities and great strengths can inspire us to emulate those qualities. On the other hand, those with serious faults can be powerful reminders of our own weaknesses and shortcomings. Confucius reminds us that we can learn much from both kinds of people: "The good points of one I copy; the bad points of the other I correct in myself."

This is a pattern of learning we should readily adopt. When people are kind and generous, that should motivate us to increase our kindness and generosity. However, when we see people acting unkindly and insensitively, that too should be incentive for us to be on guard against any unkind or insensitive impulses in ourselves. On this day, make it your intention to view every person you meet as a teacher, bringing you an important lesson. At the end of the day, review those whom you encountered, trying to determine what lessons they brought you.

THOUGHTS

Don't believe everything you think!

> *Most people believe the mind to be a mirror, more or less*
> *accurately reflecting on the world outside them, not*
> *realizing on the contrary that the mind is itself the*
> *principal element of creation.*
>
> —Rabindranath Tagore

Many thoughts can be described as "violence against yourself." Consider people whose thoughts cause them to have anxiety attacks, or the person who feels sick to his stomach or experiences chest pains because of some upsetting thoughts. If someone were to strike us in the stomach or the chest, we would rightly consider that action abusive. Yet most people do not stop to consider the abusive nature of their thinking. In the East, it is generally understood that the mind is restless, untamed, and sometimes violent. Our minds can jump from one idea to another, then another and another, without any connecting link between them, causing us a great deal of anxiety. The key is not to take our thoughts so seriously, and not to believe everything we think. To help you do this, consider these thoughts about thoughts:

- Thoughts are visitors that come our way: some are welcome, some not.
- They can be pleasant or unpleasant, helpful or hurtful, *but* they are *only* thoughts.
- Much of our turmoil is the result of permitting our mind to run rampant.

Meditation is a tool that tames the mind. Part of the meditation process is to observe our thoughts. Our thoughts are often intimidated by being observed, and they usually recede. Rather than be distracted and driven by your thoughts, simply slow yourself down and observe them. Become a detached witness to your own thoughts. Calmly let them run their course without having to respond or react to them. You will be amazed at how quickly they dissipate. Eastern sages frequently remind people that it is not the thoughts that disturb us, it is our reaction to them. The most effective way of dealing with thoughts is through meditation. Meditation helps us to tame the mind; to be aware of the thinking process without identifying with the various thoughts that the mind throws at us. Most of us are frequently in turmoil or confused or even frightened because our normal response is to react to our thoughts. That's why so many find meditation calming, relaxing, soothing, and a great source of joy and peace. In meditation we simply witness our thinking, slow down the activity of the mind, and begin to experience the deeper, more authentic self, which lies hidden beneath our mental turmoil.

Here's a simple way to begin taming the mind with meditation. Set aside ten minutes in your day. Find a quiet place where you won't be disturbed. Sit—either in a chair or on the floor—with your spine straightened. Close your eyes and begin meditating by noticing your breathing. Breathe in slowly and exhale slowly. When thoughts arise, as they will, simply observe them briefly and then return the focus to your breath. Do this for ten minutes. Try meditating daily or at least several times a week, gradually increasing your meditation time. As you become a more experienced meditator, you will learn how to merely watch the mind without getting caught up in its dramas. You will be less impacted by thoughts—less likely to regard them as "me" and more able to view them for what they are: passing thoughts. You may not notice positive results the first few times you meditate, but if you are patient, they will appear. It's not possible to meditate without receiving benefits.

TONGLEN

> *Hurting can be transformed into healing; pain into peace;*
> *a burden into a blessing.*
> —Victor M. Parachin

Tonglen is a Tibetan word meaning "breathing in and breathing out." It is a simple but deep meditative practice that empowers us to work with negative issues, transforming them into something beneficial. Tonglen can be done for yourself and for others.

Here's an example of an ideal time to do tonglen for yourself. Let's assume you've been talking with your partner or friend over some matter and a strong difference of opinion has emerged. As sometimes happens, the discussion turns into a heated argument and your friend declares: "The problem with you is that you think you know everything!" Your friend has pushed all your buttons and you're feeling sorely misunderstood, hurt, betrayed, and angry. Three steps are involved in doing a tonglen meditation. The purpose is to transform that harsh, negative emotional climate.

1. Get some privacy and become quiet. Sit briefly in meditation, reflecting on what transpired. Try to see yourself as an enlightened being, someone who is viewing the entire scene from a pure and detached perspective. You can clearly see your friend and hear the painful remark. You can also see yourself as a person who is suffering from the encounter.

Now take a few seconds to pause and prepare for completely transforming the event. During this meditative moment, some people find it helpful to see themselves in a large, white, empty room that can be painted in new colors. The room symbolizes your opportunity to create something fresh and new.

2. Breathe in the bad. Become aware of the feelings you experienced as a result of the argument with your friend: anger, hurt, fear, loneliness, misunderstanding. See those emotions as a dark puff of smoke. As you breathe in, see those emotions—the dark puff of smoke—disintegrating inside of your body. They fade away.

3. Breathe out the good. As you exhale, see yourself breathing out, not dark puffs of smoke, but bright, white, fluffy clouds. Breathe out understanding, kindness, light, and unconditional love and peace toward yourself. Essentially what a tonglen meditation teaches is to breathe in pain and breathe out compassion. You may have to do this several times before you feel its effect.

Here's how to do a tonglen meditation for someone who is suffering. Again, the same three steps are utilized.

1. Get some privacy and become quiet. Bring into your awareness a person who you know is suffering, perhaps a friend who has been diagnosed with cancer.

2. Breathe in the bad. Breathe in the person's suffering in the form of a dark puff of smoke. See the pain and smoke coming into your body where it is dissolved.

3. Breathe out the good. Exhale outward bright, white, fluffy clouds of healing love, confidence, trust, serenity, hope, and joy. As you continue to breathe in and out, visualize your friend being filled with well-being, peace, happiness, and love.

Tonglen is a way for us to confront painful emotions instead of repressing them, which only allows them to grow stronger, magnifying their power over us. By facing them directly, we are able to dissolve negative emotions, rather than allow them to distort our thinking and feeling. Make tonglen meditation a regular part of your life whenever you encounter sadness and sorrow, either in yourself or in someone else. As you do this routinely, your tonglen practice will become stronger and more confident.

TRANSCENDING

ELIMINATING EMOTIONAL MASOCHISM.

> *In the end these things matter most:*
> *How well did you love?*
> *How fully did you love?*
> *How deeply did you learn to let go?*
> —THE BUDDHA

A long, long time ago, there were two holy men traveling together through the countryside. They came upon a beautiful young woman sitting and sobbing by the side of a stream. Concerned, one of the monks asked her what was wrong. "I need to cross this river but I can't swim and I am afraid of drowning," she explained. Without hesitation, the monk picked up the woman, carrying her to the other side of the stream, where he gently put her down. She thanked him profusely.

As the monks walked away, the second monk turned to the first, demanding, "How could you do such a thing? We have taken vows of poverty and chastity. It is forbidden even to talk to a woman, let alone touch one."

The first monk listened and succinctly replied, "When I came to the other side of the river, I put her down. Why are you still carrying her?"

That story raises this question for us today: *What are you carrying around that you should have put down and left behind long ago?* An incredible number of people go through their entire lives carrying feelings of regret, guilt, anger, disappointment, rage, and even hate. Unwittingly they practice an emotional masochism that continues to haunt and hurt them. By not letting go, they remain trapped inside prisons of their own construction. Today, resolve to be like the monk who put the beautiful woman down and moved on with his life. Don't carry your emotional baggage any longer. Let it go!

TREASURE

FINDING THE TREASURE WITHIN.

> *At the center of your being you have the answer;*
> *you know who you are and you know what you want.*
> —LAO TZU

Tourists visiting Bangkok, Thailand, often take tours of the city's many famous Buddhist temples. There is one in particular that leaves a lasting impression, known as the Temple of the Golden Buddha. The temple itself is quite small by Buddhist standards, measuring thirty feet by thirty feet. Inside, however, is a ten-and-a-half-foot, solid-gold Buddha weighing over two and a half tons. Its value is in the hundreds of millions of dollars. That treasure was unknown for centuries.

In 1957, a group of monks wanted to move a clay Buddha from their temple to a new location, because their monastery had to be relocated to make room for a new highway through Bangkok. When the crane began to lift the giant statue, it started to crack. The head monk, concerned about the crack, as well as the gathering rain, had the Buddha lowered back to the ground and covered with a large canvas tarp to protect it from the rain.

Later that evening he went to check on the statue, shining his flashlight under the tarp to be sure it was staying dry. As the light reached the crack, he noticed a little gleam shining back. Taking a closer look, he wondered if there was something underneath the clay. Using a chisel and hammer, he began to carefully chip away at the clay. As he knocked off pieces, the little gleam grew brighter and brighter. After hours of labor, he and his monks stood face to face with an extraordinary solid-gold Buddha.

Historians speculate that several hundred years earlier, as the Burmese army was about to invade Thailand (then called Siam), the Siamese monks covered their precious golden Buddha with an outer covering of clay to keep their treasure from being looted by the Burmese. Unfortunately, all the monks were killed in the conflict, and their well-hidden golden Buddha remained a secret until 1957.

That story is a perfect illustration of the Eastern teaching that inside each one of us is a treasure of divinity: perfect and complete love, wisdom, courage, insight, joy, and peace. Sadly, that treasure is often covered and concealed. We need to chip away at the external covering in order to discover our true essence.

TUMO

THE POWER OF MIND OVER BODY.

To the mind that is still, the whole universe surrenders.
—Lao Tzu

Incredibly, Tibetan monks can meditate for hours on end in freezing temperatures, clad only in thin garments or even completely naked. In spite of the high mountain altitudes where temperatures drop well below freezing, they are able to maintain a comfortable body temperature. They harness the power of the mind over the body through a meditation exercise called *tumo*. Tumo is the practice of warming oneself without fire. Across the centuries, it became imperative for monks who spent harsh Tibetan winters meditating in caves to do this in order to survive. This practice has been studied, documented, and verified by numerous Western researchers.

For many years, the method used and perfected by Tibetan monks was a great mystery to the few Westerners who visited Tibet and learned of the practice. However, as more and more Westerners became interested in Tibetan Buddhism and traveled to the region to study it firsthand, the techniques for this ancient practice became better known. One of the first Europeans to penetrate Tibet was a remarkable woman named Alexandra David-Neel (1868-1969). She spoke Tibetan fluently, and, by disguising herself alternately as a man or an old beggar woman, spent a dozen years in and around Tibet, considered at the time to be a "forbidden kingdom." Specifically, she studied the art of tumo (or body heat control), which later saved her life when she was lost and roaming in the frozen Himalayas. In one of her books, Ms. David-Neel outlines the ten mental stages for practicing tumo. These are presented here only as an example of the power of meditation to control the body. The ten stages may be briefly described as follows:

1. The central artery of the body is visualized as thin—like the thinnest thread or hair—yet filled with a growing flame fanned by a current of air produced by the breath.

2. The artery increases in size, becoming as large as the little finger.

3. It continues to increase, appearing to be the size of an arm.

4. That flaming artery fills the whole body.

5. The bodily form ceases to be perceived, and the flaming artery encompasses the whole world, leaving the meditator feeling that he or she is being washed over by glowing waves of an ocean of fire.

Those five steps motivate the body to generate heat in freezing temperatures. Coming out of that meditative state is done gradually and follows this reverse order:

6. The fiery waves recede sinking lower and lower.

7. The artery is visualized as the size of an arm, with the fire enclosed within the artery.

8. The artery decreases to the size of a little finger.

9. It becomes as thin as a hair.

10. It entirely disappears and the fire ceases to be perceived.

While these steps make the practice of tumo appear rather simple, it takes monks, guided by a master, many months to perfect. Tumo is a dramatic example of the power that meditation can generate to control the mind and body. While we may not be particularly interested in generating physical warmth this way, we ought to be mindful that meditation can be equally effective in reducing stress, increasing confidence, triggering deep insights, and generating courage to live in healthier and more positive ways.

UNDERSTANDING

UNDERSTANDING THAT YOU ARE NOT YOUR BODY.

> *Do you not know that your body is a temple of the Holy*
> *Spirit, who is in you...?*
>
> —1 CORINTHIANS 6:19

People who have a highly developed and highly sensitive spirituality often find themselves overwhelmed to be in a body and to have to live in this world. I have often wondered if those whose birth was difficult and labor lengthy are simply souls who were trying to delay their decision to be here. Similarly, I have wondered if babies who are born prematurely and whose first weeks are a struggle between life and death, may be souls who are not ready to choose life, and who are battling between staying and leaving.

In the East, it is commonly understood and taught that a person is not his or her body; that the body is simply a physical entity that contains and carries the true spirit. St. Paul sounds decidedly Hindu when he asks: "Do you not know that your body is a temple of the Holy Spirit, who is in you?"(1Cor. 6:19). Like all Eastern teachers, St. Paul is aware that inside the body is the true person, a spiritual entity whose essence is divinity. Eastern thought holds that death is not a dead end; it is merely a release from the body, which can, over time, become a tomb or prison for the spirit. The body dies, but the soul never ceases to exist.

Although the concept that "you are not your body" may appear foreign here in the West, there are times when it readily resonates with our experience. For example, people who have aged will often look into a mirror and exclaim to themselves: "Who is that old, bald man?" or "Who is that old, gray-haired woman?" Or consider a young woman who was born with deformities. Her left arm is a short stub with a small hand and three fingers. "I am not my body," she says. These individuals have difficulty recognizing themselves in the mirror because that view does not convey who they truly are. Inside is not an old, bald man or an old, gray-haired woman. Inside is not a young woman born with deformities. Inside is a person who still thinks and experiences life in a vibrant, enthusiastic way, regardless of how they appear in the mirror.

The Eastern insistence that we are not our bodies is difficult to embrace in the West because the media bombard our culture with images of perfect bodies that most of us can never have. Yet, we often receive reminders that we are not our bodies. These reminders come in the form of resistance or even repulsion to events occurring in our world. If you find yourself at a place where you are simply unable to read one more horrible news headline—a rape, a murder, a war, a weather disaster that claims many lives—try to consider the Eastern idea that the real you (not your body), that divine part of you which is pure love, pure compassion, pure kindness, pure goodness, is severely reacting to the sordid reality of this planet. That divine essence who is the authentic person may, in fact, be crying out and saying, "I can't stand this." It is a small taste, perhaps, of what God must feel when God looks at the planet and sees the great inhumanity and injustice that constantly take place.

Finally, since the body houses or contains the real you, the authentic person who is part of God, we ought to treat the body with reverence and care. That means being certain that the body receives the right nourishment, the right fluids, and the right balance between work and play, rest, and exercise. Because it contains and carries the real you, it needs to be properly nourished and nurtured. As the Buddha says: "The body is precious. It is our vehicle for awakening. Treat it with care."

VIRTUES

THE VALUE OF VIRTUE.

A (wise person) is good to people who are good.
She is also good to people who are not good.
This is true goodness.

—LAO TZU

In ancient China there lived a beautiful woman who served in the court of the local prince. Her beauty was noticed by the prince, who began to favor and court her. Once when the beautiful woman's mother was sick, she was so concerned that she immediately went to visit her mother, using the prince's carriage without first asking for permission. According to the laws of the province, no one could ride in the prince's carriage without permission. The penalty for breaking that law was severe: the rider was to have his or her foot cut off. However, when the prince found out what she had done, he publicly praised the beautiful woman for her devotion and compassion: "Imagine risking such a severe punishment for her mother," he said to his advisors.

On another occasion, while the beautiful woman and the prince were walking in the royal garden, the woman picked a ripe peach and, finding it delicious, gave it to the prince to finish. Again, the prince praised her publicly, saying, "How much she must love me to forget her own pleasure and to share the peach with me."

However, as the years went by and the woman's beauty began to fade, she fell out of favor with the prince. One day when she did something the prince didn't like, he criticized her publicly saying, "I remember how she once took my carriage without permission. And another time she gave me a peach that she had already bitten into."

This story is about virtues such as faithfulness, unconditional love, and loyalty, all of which are absent in the prince. While the woman is beautiful, he is mesmerized, appreciative, attentive, understanding. When her physical beauty fades—as it does in all of us, the prince included—he becomes critical, scornful, and dismissive. A virtue is a character trait valued as being good. Sadly, the prince exhibits a lack of moral virtue in this story. Perhaps the lesson to glean from this ancient episode is to look at ourselves and be certain that we are not like the prince, individuals who set others aside when they are no longer useful to us.

# WORDS

USING OUR WORDS WISELY.

> *Cold words freeze people, and hot words scorch them, and*
> *bitter words make them bitter, and wrathful words make*
> *them wrathful. Kind words . . . soothe, and quiet, and*
> *comfort the hearer.*
>
> —BLAISE PASCAL

The third step in Buddhism's Eightfold Path is "right speech." Ancient religious philosophers knew the power inherent in every word spoken, and they consistently urged their disciples to use their words wisely and compassionately. That lesson is clearly conveyed in this story of an ancient king who dreamed that all his teeth had fallen out. Troubled by his dream, he sent for a wise man from the kingdom to interpret the dream. The man listened to the king's dream, thought about it briefly, and then delivered this interpretation: "Your Highness, the dream means that all your relatives will die and you will be left alone."

The king was furious at the man's interpretation, and demanded that he be removed and banned from the palace at once. He then called for a second wise man to come and interpret the dream. This wise man also listened to the king's dream, pondered for a moment, and then offered this interpretation: "Rejoice, O King! The dream means that you will live many more years. In fact, you will outlive all your relatives. Long live the king!" This interpretation so pleased the king that he gave the wise man a large purse of gold.

Look closely at the interpretations of the two wise men. They essentially made identical predictions. However, there was an enormous difference in *how* they delivered the message. As a result, there was an enormous difference in *how* the message was received. The moral of that story is clear: it's not merely *what* we say, but *how* we say it that counts. The fact is that the words we use can arouse anger or appreciation, hostility or harmony, despair or delight. This day as you speak to those around you, pay close attention to the words you use. Be certain that your words heal not hurt, inspire not injure, bless not burden.

X: The mathematical symbol for the unknown

HAVE A BEGINNER'S MIND.

> *In the beginner's mind there are many possibilities,*
> *but in the expert's there are few.*
> —SHUNRYU SUZUKI

In Eastern thought, the empty mind is the open mind, ready for new insights, new concepts, new ways of living and responding. The empty mind is also referred to as a "beginner's mind," because in the beginner's mind there are a multitude of possibilities. However, in the "expert's" mind or the "experienced" mind, the options and possibilities are considerably reduced. Shunryu Suzuki (1905-1971), a Japanese Zen master who came to the United States in 1958, founding several Zen centers, was stating the importance of remaining open to the unknown; of adopting a life stance of constant learning and growth. Most of us are easily frustrated by individuals who "think they know everything." The beginner's mind is one of openness and innocence.

Developing a beginner's mind is at the heart of this well-known Eastern story. A highly learned scholar visited a Zen master. Initially he came to inquire about becoming enlightened. However, all he did was talk incessantly to the Zen master. As the professor talked on and on, the master began to pour him a cup of tea. Once the tea cup was full, the Zen master continued pouring and the tea flowed over the cup, onto the table, and onto the floor. "Stop pouring!" shouted the professor. Continuing to pour tea, the Zen master told the professor, "This cup is like your mind. There is absolutely no room for anything new."

So, Shunryu Suzuki's statement about having a beginner's mind is both a haunting one and a challenging one. Haunting because it identifies a fault which we easily fall into, that of assuming far too much. It is challenging, because it asks us to make this assessment: *Do I convey attitudes that indicate I know everything? Do I honestly have a beginner's mind? Am I open to the unknown so that my learning and growing can deepen?* Today let the letter "X," which is the mathematical symbol for the unknown, be your guide. Don't be a "know-it-all." Free your mind and spirit to embrace the unknown. Open yourself to the opportunities that emerge when you maintain a beginner's mind.

XENOPHILIA

HAVING AN OPEN HEART FOR THE STRANGER.

> *Do not forget to entertain strangers, for by so doing some*
> *people have entertained angels without knowing it.*
> —HEBREWS 13:2

Xenophilia is an unusual word which simply means "love for the stranger." The dictionary definition of a xenophile is someone attracted to "that which is foreign, especially to foreign peoples or cultures." This quality is frequently seen in Tibetan Buddhist monks, who commonly greet strangers visiting their temples with this question: "Welcome friend, from what noble tradition do you come?" Similarly, I had as neighbors a wonderful Hindu family from India. The grandfather, who walked daily through our neighborhood, always greeted me by folding his palms, as if in prayer, and saying *namaste*. As noted above, *namaste* is a common Eastern greeting meaning "The divine within me salutes the divine within you."

Interestingly, Jewish rabbis also stress the importance of having the open spirit of a xenophile. They tell of an old rabbi who asked his pupils how they could distinguish when night ended and the day begins.

"Could it be," asked one of the students, "when you can see an animal in the distance and tell whether it's a sheep or a dog?"

"No," said the rabbi.

Another student asked, "Is it when you can look at a tree in the distance and tell whether it's a fig tree or a peach tree?"

"No," said the rabbi again.

"Then when is it?" the frustrated students demanded.

"It is when you can look on the face of any man or woman and see that it is your sister or brother. Because if you cannot see this, it is still night."

Healthy spirituality means the daily practice of xenophilia—having love and respect for the stranger or foreigner whom we encounter. Doing so cuts down considerably on nationalistic chauvinism and regional parochialism, whereby we perceive ourselves and our culture as superior to that of others. The practice of xenophilia eliminates harmful distinctions between "us and them," "we and they." It moves us from an unhealthy preoccupation with the self toward an awareness of the goodness present in others.

 YOGA

DISCIPLINING THE BODY TO DISCIPLINE THE MIND.

The obstacles that distract thought are disease, apathy,
doubt, carelessness, indolence, dissipation, false vision,
failure to attain a firm basis in yoga, and restlessness.
—PATANJALI

Every year, more and more people engage in yoga as exercise. Today yoga classes can be found not only at yoga studios, but in health clubs, schools, churches, and hotels. It is done by men and women, children and teens, the young and the elderly, and can be found in large cities as well as small rural communities. The yoga postures practiced in the West are actually only one of eight "limbs" of Eastern yoga philosophy. An Indian sage named Patanjali developed the eight limbs of yoga, a sophisticated method for transforming human awareness. (See the next section on "Yoga, Part 2," for more information on Patanjali and the eight limbs.)

In spite of its growing popularity and availability, many still view yoga as an esoteric Indian activity. For many, the image of yoga is that of thin vegetarians with weightless bodies that they twist and bend into bizarre shapes. Some mistakenly view yoga as an Eastern religion that is not compatible with their own Christianity. Here are some frequently asked questions about yoga.

What is yoga?

The word *yoga* comes from the Sanskrit word *yuj*, and is translated as "union." Developed in India more than five thousand years ago, yoga is a system designed to energize and strengthen the mind and increase body awareness. Those who practice yoga today engage in poses that lead to better physical health and psychological well-being. It is not uncommon to hear yoga practitioners say they enjoy a greater sense of inner peace as a result of their yoga practice. A woman who practices yoga is called a *yogi*ni while a man is called a *yogi*.

Is yoga a religion?

Yoga is not a religion. Yoga has its roots in India, and those who have contributed most to its development have come from the Hindu faith. However, many people who engage in yoga find that they develop an increased sense of spiritual awareness, connection, and compassion. This seems to happen regardless of whether they are persons of faith, and regardless of what spiritual beliefs they hold.

Do I have to be religious or spiritual to practice yoga?

Anyone can practice yoga and everyone is welcome. There is no requirement that participants have any religious or spiritual outlook. Yet many who begin to practice yoga say they experience subtle shifts in attitudes and thoughts, often coming to a greater appreciation of life's spiritual aspects. Similarly, those who come to yoga with spiritual inclinations find that the practice deepens and enriches their own faith.

What are the benefits of yoga?

In the East, the practicing of yoga postures is an aid to meditation. When the body has been stretched and exercised, it is less restless (Patanjali's term), and the mind is therefore more free to focus on meditation. In addition, yoga is very good medicine—its health benefits are vast and various. They include stress reduction, increased flexibility, calmness of mind, relief of chronic pain, easing of depression, as well as improved cardiovascular, respiratory, and circulatory health. Yoga is regarded by both teachers and students as a highly effective way to integrate body, mind, and spirit.

Why are so many people taking yoga classes?

If you were to take a poll of people in a yoga class, asking them, "Why are you here?" the answers would likely differ with each person. People come to yoga bringing a vast array of emotional, mental, and physical needs. Some come for stress reduction and pain relief. Others come to gain a deeper sense of inner peace and greater awareness. Still others like yoga for the physical workout it provides.

Can I take yoga if I'm not flexible?

You do not need the flexibility of a gymnast to participate in yoga. Actually, yoga is ideal for those whose flexibility is limited. By practicing yoga regularly you will lengthen your muscles and experience more flexibility. This, in turn, can prevent a variety of injuries.

Is it necessary to be a vegetarian to practice yoga?

No. Probably most people who do yoga are not vegetarians. Many teachers do stress the importance of treating the body well, and that often implies replacing a meat-based diet with one that is more dependent on fruits, grains, and vegetables.

However, vegetarianism is never forced or imposed upon students of yoga. It is a personal decision.

What is a guru and do I need one?

A guru is a teacher rich in spiritual wisdom and knowledge who becomes a spiritual mentor or coach. You don't need a guru to participate in yoga. Whether or not you need one for your own spiritual growth is a personal decision. Most yoga teachers are not gurus; they are simply individuals who have taken the time to be trained in teaching yoga.

Is meditation part of a yoga class?

Most classes begin and end with a few minutes of silence. The purpose of this time of silence is to still the mind; it is a powerful balance for our overactive minds. Taking a few moments of quiet at the beginning and end of a yoga class encourages relaxation, increases awareness, and enhances mental clarity.

Why do some yoga classes chant *Om?*

Not every yoga session includes chanting. The practice of chanting varies from teacher to teacher and from studio to studio. *Om* is an ancient mantra first used by Indian sages. It is considered a sacred syllable, consisting in Sanskrit of three sounds—(a), (u), and (m)—and is traditionally chanted either at the beginning or end of a class, or sometimes both. In Eastern thought, *Om* symbolizes ultimate reality; chanting the syllable is viewed as a way for humans to sense their connection to something much larger.

YOGA (Part 2)

UNDERSTANDING THE DEEPER DIMENSIONS OF YOGA.

Yoga is the process of becoming free from limited definitions of the field of consciousness.

—YOGA SUTRA OF PATANJALI I. 2,3

Sometime between 200 BCE and 200 CE there lived a wandering physician and mystic called Patanjali. Throughout India and other parts of the East, Patanjali is a highly respected and revered figure. Because of his collection of 195 concise proverbs or sayings, known as the *Yoga Sutra of Patanjali*, Patanjali is regarded as the founder or, more accurately, the organizer of yoga. Without his *Sutras* we might not have the gift of yoga. Surprisingly, however, in his 195 *Sutras,* there is not one description of a posture or *asana*. For Patanjali, the term *yoga* (which means "union") stands for a sophisticated philosophical, ethical, and moral framework for living a meaningful, purposeful life.

In other words, you can't just go to a yoga class, spend an hour or so doing various postures, and then leave to cheat on your taxes, mistreat your partner, lie to colleagues, or be rude, cruel, or indifferent. The true purpose of yoga is to promote spiritual and moral growth. To help all of us achieve such growth, Patanjali writes about the eight "limbs" or the Eightfold Path of yoga—keep in mind as you read that these limbs are not linear, but are intertwined, much like the branches of a tree in a dense forest:

1. Yama: This limb deals with issues of personal integrity, ethics, and moral choices, specifically: nonviolence, truthfulness, non-stealing, non-lust, and freedom from greed and hoarding.

2. Niyama: The second limb focuses on inner discipline and how we treat ourselves—our bodies, our minds, and our spirits. Niyama bears a striking similarity to the philosophy expressed by the Christian apostle Paul, who wrote: "Your body is a temple of the Holy Spirit . . . honor God with your body" (1 Cor. 6:19). Emphases included in this limb are: cleanliness; eating of fresh, healthy food; cultivating contentment, tranquility, and stability; austerity or self-discipline of body, mind, and speech; study of sacred scriptures in order to become inspired and to grow in spiritual knowledge; and devotion to the divine by whatever name (Buddha, Christ, Krishna, Allah) you call that divinity.

3. Asana: This limb is yoga as most of us in the West know it—postures we do to exercise, stretch, and strengthen the body. For Patanjali, however, the purpose of asana is preparation for meditation. An exercised, strong body is better suited for lengthy periods of sitting still.

4. Pranayama: This limb deals with breath control. It consists of techniques designed to give us greater control over the respiratory process. The basic pattern of pranayama is inhalation, retention of breath, and exhalation. Many yogis teach that our lives are not measured by the number of days or years but by the number of breaths. Proper breathing is also an aid to deepen meditation.

5. *Pratyahara:* The fifth limb outlines the importance of withdrawing the senses from the external world in order to direct our attention inwardly. Practicing pratyahara means being able to focus and concentrate, regardless of other stimuli coming our way. In the yoga room, it means focusing on doing a pose, without being distracted by a fly on your leg. In a meeting or conference, pratyahara means being able to concentrate on what is transpiring, rather than being distracted by a telephone ringing or someone walking down the hall.

6. *Dharana:* This limb is the discipline that teaches us to focus the mind on one point or image, such as a candle flame, a flower, or a mantra. Unlike the fifth limb, which trains us to dismiss outside distractions, dharana trains us to deal with the internal distractions of the mind.

7. *Dhyana:* The seventh limb is a very high state of meditation, done without any "props" such as a candle flame, flower, or mantra. It is being ultimately focused, but without a focal point. Yogis say this one is true meditation, as opposed to mere concentration. The difference, yogis would say, is this: "If you have awareness of a distraction, you are only concentrating, not meditating."

8. *Samadhi:* This is the final and deepest stage of meditation, one whereby the meditator merges with the divine and completely transcends the self. There is a profound realization of the divine and connection to all living things. Distinctions are completely gone. All is one. Some yogis call this "union with God." The Bible refers to this state as "the peace of God, which transcends all understanding" (Phil. 4:7).

YUGA

WHAT KIND OF PERSON ARE YOU?

Take away love and our earth is a tomb.
—ROBERT BROWNING

Have you ever had the feeling that there is often more wrong than right in our world? Or have you ever entertained the idea that there is more evil than good out there? If so, you are very much in line with the Hindu philosophy of time, known as *yuga*.

The term *yuga* is a Sanskrit word to describe great expanses of time. According to Hindu philosophy, the entire universe runs on a cyclical pattern of four *yugas,* which roll by one after another. The four *yugas* are enormous lengths of time:
- *Krita Yuga,* which equates to approximately 1,728,000 years.
- *Treta Yuga*, which is 1,296,000 years.
- *Dvapara Yuga*, which runs 864,000 years.
- *Kali Yuga*, which is 432,000 years.

At the end of the *Kali Yuga* era, the world comes to an end, and the cycle begins all over again. In the first era, *Krita Yuga,* all persons are pure of heart and people live in complete peace and harmony. In the second era, *Treta Yuga,* one quarter of the people lose their goodness: seventy-five percent are good and twenty-five percent have tendencies for evil. By the time the third era, *Dvapara Yuga,* rolls around, it's fifty-fifty. In the *Kali Yuga,* or fourth era, only one-quarter of the population is altruistic, kind, loving, compassionate. The other three-quarters are at their worst behavior. During this era, the world comes to some kind of end, and then the cycle starts all over again, beginning with *Krita Yuga.*

The news gets worse. According to Hindu philosophy, we are currently living in the last and most challenging era, when the majority of people lack civility, kindness, and compassion. In addition, the *Kali Yuga* era began only about five thousand years ago, meaning that there is still a long period of time when the majority of people will be at their worst. One of the Hindu Scriptures, the *Vishnu Purana,* describes the *Kali Yuga* era in this disturbingly accurate way:

> In the Kali Yuga, there will be numerous rulers vying with each other. They will have no character. Violence, falsehood and wickedness will be the order of the day. Piety and good nature will dwindle slowly . . . Passion and lust will be the only attraction between the sexes. Women will be objects of sensual pleasure. Dishonesty will be the bottom line of subsistence. Learned people will be ridiculed and put to shame; the word of the wealthy person will be the only law.

The Eastern view of time helps make some sense of our current reality, in which there is so much hatred, conflict, strife, and war in our world. And closer to home, that philosophy of time can also help us understand why so many people around us seem to be difficult, obnoxious, unkind, even dangerous. If seventy-five percent of us are at our worst, then it is easy to understand why we live cautiously and fearfully, and why we feel hurt so often. Robert Browning is quite right: "Take away love and our earth is a tomb."

Rather than allowing this knowledge to make us discouraged and despairing about our world, we should be motivated to delve more deeply into ethical and spiritual practices. We ought to be certain that whenever we speak and act, we are doing so as members of the twenty-five percent of the population whose hearts are pure, good, kind, loving, and compassionate. Those who are grounded and centered become an oasis of hope for humanity. They are the candle in the darkness, showing others how to act and live. So today, ask yourself this important question: *by my words and actions, where would my family, friends, colleagues, and even strangers place me—in the seventy-five percent with impure hearts, or among the twenty-five percent who are loving, kind, and pure of heart?*

 ZEN

PRACTICING ZEN AWARENESS

> *To study Zen is to study the self.*
> *To study the self is to forget the self.*
> *Once we stop focusing on ourselves, the*
> *whole world opens up to us in a new way.*
>
> —ROBERT E. KENNEDY

Here are some quick facts about Zen:

- It is a Buddhist sect imported from China into Japan sometime in the twelfth century.
- Teachings are transmitted from master to disciple through the use of riddles or paradoxes called *koans*.
- The word "Zen" derives from a Sanskrit word *dhyana*, meaning meditation.
- Zen has no rigid doctrines, rejects veneration of images, is suspicious of scriptures, and advocates self-realization.
- Self-realization can be sudden or gradual, and comes as a result of *zazen*, or meditation.

• Zen emphasizes the vital importance of understanding that "now" is the only time and "here" is the only place.

• Zen was immensely popular among Japan's warrior class.

• During the twentieth century, Zen was introduced and became popular in the West primarily through the writings of D. T. Suzuki.

• Zen methods of meditation and reflection are increasingly being used by Christians.

• Because Zen is not strictly a philosophy nor a religion, Zen can be adapted by people of varying religious or non-religious backgrounds.

• Only through direct personal meditation and vigilant awareness can human delusion arising from greed, anger and ignorance be overcome.

Those are some quick facts about Zen, but the best way to approach it is by reading Zen stories, all of which teach important lessons about life and about Zen philosophy. Here are two stories to whet your appetite. (If you'd like more, visit a bookstore and select a book of Zen tales.)

After ten years of apprenticeship, Tenno achieved the rank of Zen teacher. One rainy day, he went to visit the famous master Nan-in. When he walked in, the master greeted him with a question: "Did you leave your wooden clogs and umbrella on the porch?"

"Yes," Tenno replied.

"Tell me," the master continued, "did you place your umbrella to the left of your shoes, or to the right?"

Tenno did not know the answer, and realized that he had not yet attained full awareness. So he became Nan-in's apprentice, and studied under him for ten more years.

The lesson in that story is fairly obvious, and very indicative of the Zen approach to life and learning: even though he had already studied Zen for ten years, Tenno's awareness of himself and his world still needed more work. Perhaps he wondered to himself, "How many other experiences in life do I let slip by me?" Tenno understood that becoming truly aware requires great effort and training, and so he continued his apprenticeship.

The second story is about two monks who were washing their bowls in the river when they noticed a drowning scorpion. One monk immediately scooped it up and set it upon the bank, getting stung in the process. He went back to washing his bowl, and again the scorpion fell in. The monk saved the scorpion and again was stung. The other monk asked him, "Friend, why do you continue to save the scorpion when you know its nature is to sting?"

"Because," the monk replied, "to save it is my nature."

People who read that story can find various Zen meanings in it. One person may see in it the monk's self-awareness as a compassionate person, extending that compassion to all life forms. Because he has been practicing compassion, probably for years, it has become "second nature" to him. The monk chooses to save a life and endure the sting as the price of living by a higher principle. Another person, perhaps one who is struggling in life, can find personal comfort and courage from that story because it is a reminder that being engaged in life can bring pain. In spite of our best intentions, life can hurt—we lose jobs, relationships end, illness strikes. This is natural; it ought to be expected and taken for what it is.